11.9.79

Reading
for the
point

WILLIAM J. KERRIGAN

Fullerton College

HARCOURT BRACE JOVANOVICH, INC.

NEW YORK   SAN DIEGO   CHICAGO   SAN FRANCISCO   ATLANTA

William J. Kerrigan, *Reading for the Point*

Copyright © 1979 by Harcourt Brace Jovanovich, Inc.

ISBN: 0-15-575640-0

Library of Congress Catalog Card Number: 78-71336

Printed in the United States of America

Copyrights and Acknowledgments appear on page 141, which constitutes a continuation of the copyright page.

letter to the instructor

Evidently, it is forgivable only in a child to say, "The Emperor has no clothes." So if I say practically the same thing about college reading, is it unforgivable in me? Let's see what *you* would say.

Be honest. As a college freshman, did you understand the selections in the assigned textbook of readings? Perhaps, like some candid English instructors I know of, you'll admit that you didn't. But perhaps you did, and furthermore assumed—falsely, it would seem—that all your classmates understood them, too.

But in either case, do you *now* honestly think that freshmen can read the selections that are thrown at them—whether an article from *Commonweal*, an editorial from *Field and Stream*, a feature from the *Wall Street Journal*, a review from *Commentary*, even a short essay from *TV Guide*? The a priori evidence is against that assumption: first, in the traditional estimate of freshman abilities, only 5 percent of them matched the A you got, while a full 50 percent rated as C students, and 25 percent below that. Today quite 50 percent of them are still C students, no matter what grades they may be receiving. Furthermore, reading scores on college entrance examinations have fallen substantially and are still falling. True, educators have dealt with this decline by explaining it away, so let's turn to a posteriori evidence, a passage from *TV Guide*, a publication of truly massive circulation, to test your own students on. In this excerpt from the issue of April 29, 1978, chosen pretty much at random, the magazine is describing the television industry as "a patient . . . badly shaken."

Convulsions of programming: Some observers complain that this has been, if not the worst, certainly the most chaotic season ever for television. Erratic scheduling leaves viewers bewildered; they flip through pages of *TV Guide* in search of their favorite show. Where is it? *Behavioral problems:* Decline in aggression is followed by excessive interest in sex, alternating with episodes of dullness. *Dropsy:* Nielsen studies revealed some decline in TV viewing at beginning of season, causing rapid rise in blood pressure; but latest findings suggest condition not malignant. *Paralysis:* Producers, writers, rival networks, and actors all wait anxiously to see what Dr. Fred Silverman will prescribe for NBC. *Compulsive overachievement:* Despite record earnings, networks suffer from pressure sores; each has unquenchable desire to be "No. 1."

First, give them a vocabulary test: Skipping the purely medical terminology, see if they know these words: *convulsions, chaotic, erratic, bewildered, decline, aggression, excessive, alternating, episodes, malignant, paralysis, prescribe, compulsive, despite, record earnings, unquenchable.*

Second, comprehension: What have bewildered viewers got to do with erratic scheduling? And erratic scheduling to do with the chaotic season? Have them explain the meaning of television's "decline in aggression . . . followed by an excessive interest in sex, alternating with episodes of dullness." What does the relationship between record earnings and a desire to be "No. 1" mean: are the two the same, or is this a contrast or contradiction?

An experienced and realistic teacher may not have to give the test in order to learn that few if any students can pass it creditably. But he or she may argue that the passage chosen does not constitute a fair test: there are other parts of *TV Guide* that students *can* read. In presenting such a passage (by no means an isolated one), the editors of *TV Guide* may admittedly be living in a fool's paradise. (They are not alone there.) But can your students even make sense of the whole front page of today's paper? Make a similar test. Go ahead. Then *you* tell me about the emperor's clothes.

"Well then," you may say, "half my regular freshman English students belong back in one of our remedial reading classes." More than half. "But the scheduling difficulties! Administrators would never permit it." No, they wouldn't. So what's to be done?

You can teach your students to read. Yes, you can, and you may feel that you should, if you believe it is a moral or humanitarian duty of teachers to prepare their charges for what lies ahead of them in life and if, moreover, you feel that learning to read is inseparably bound to learning to write, the two being but the opposite sides of the same coin, the precious metal of which is thinking.

You can, I insist, teach your students to read. Many of our freshmen, having pursued mathematics courses step by step through grade and high school, are now succeeding in college mathematics courses as sophisticated as calculus. *Those same freshmen* are performing in English on what has been measured as the sixth-grade level. Having realized that their mathematics teachers' success is simply the result of an ordered, step-by-step process, I have undertaken to produce a college reading textbook that, like mathematics texts, proceeds step by step to explain the elements of reading.

Is it hard for you to believe that you and I together, using this book, can improve significantly your students' reading abilities? It shouldn't be hard for you to believe it, any more than it should be hard to believe that it *must* be done, as already amply indicated by both national statistics and your own tests of your students. No, it's not hard to believe, but *hard to do!* That, in all honesty, I must admit. For the same students who over the years have worked their way patiently line by line through problems in long division and then fractions in grade school, then algebra and geometry in high school, have been persuaded that no such slow, patient, line-by-line problems need be worked in English! No! "English" in some cases has meant watching *The Guns of Navarone* in a darkened classroom, or discussing "opinions."

But experience shows that the consequent resistance can be overcome, that a dawning light can begin to dispel the darkness, and that order can be imposed on chaos. Of course we must first admit, with all the candor of the child viewing the emperor, that the darkness and chaos do exist.

After training, student *writers* can perform convincingly. They have a vocabulary fairly adequate to the expression of their thoughts, which are about things that they have adequately learned (if they can be kept from writing on matters that they know nothing about). They have an adequate way of explaining, of making a point, of arguing for the truth. But when they turn to reading, they meet what can only be called a foreign vocabulary and constant references to a world familiar to educated people but unknown to these students. Thus vocabulary—especially the capitalized nouns, wherein they glimpse the shores of that new world—remains a constant problem that this book faces as well as it can be faced. Plot will carry the students along through stories within their reach, and they will gather facts from articles of information according to their needs. But when they turn to explanatory prose, which is the particular business of this book, they find a way of explaining, of making a point, of arguing, that they cannot follow—a way that typically involves the progress of thought through contrasts, the signaling of a point through position or some other device of emphasis, the validating of a second concept by what a first one has established. Thus the students miss the point—in fact, may not even realize that a point is being made. And there is nothing worse than missing the point.

Because of these inadequacies in students' reading, this book systematically takes up, as it must, not only pointedness through contrast or through devices of emphasis, but illation, or the process of drawing conclusions and making inferences—the very point of *point*. Certain essays are used as working material, and if at first you are dismayed to find essays "interrupted" by commentary (not too frequently, even so), bear in mind that the working material—the essays used *as examples*—is included not for its own sake but precisely for the sake of the commentary. Otherwise, we put the cart before the horse and are back to a book of "readings," instead of a book on reading whereby, methodically, students are taught to minimally comprehend the explanatory prose that they will have to cope with in life. Indeed, the tendency of students to read on without understanding is precisely what must be checked.

To be sure, *uninterrupted* readings appear at the end of the book, where the students, having learned as much *about* reading as they can, are put on their own. There, *what* is read assumes importance along with *how* it is read. I am not denying humanistic values to freshman English; I only argue that, before they can get at those values, students must learn to read. I well remember struggling through Demosthenes' *Peri tou stephanou:* its magnificent oratory was lost on me because the simple Greek of Xenophon, with its comparatively primitive syntax and connectives, was all I knew, leaving me unprepared for Demosthenes' language. Comparatively, I knew only as much Greek as the average college entrant does English. Confront that individual with a chapter of Newman's *Idea of a University* and he or she will be lost in it from the first line. Alas, I cannot read Demosthenes to this day, but I can read Plato. And our average student may never be adequate to *The Idea of a University,* but may be able, in some translation, to read Plato—say his *Ion.*

A final word. If you believe, as I do, that reading and writing are inseparable, you may want to know about a companion to this volume, my *Writing to the Point,* which is in its second edition. For if students—if *we*—can learn to read for the point and write to the point, we will find ourselves on the high road to becoming educated citizens. And that, after all, is precisely the point, is it not?

WILLIAM J. KERRIGAN

contents

chapter fourteen

reading
for the
point

chapter

The purpose of this book is to help you with the reading you will have to do for your college classes and for your life later on, as a person who has had college training.

No doubt you already have a good start in reading. Certainly you have had practice. You studied your textbooks in high school, and the stories, poems, and plays you were given in high school English classes. Outside school, you read whatever interested you in books, magazine articles, or parts of the daily newspaper.

Thinking back, you can even see that your good start was more than a start; it was constant progress. The more you read, the better able you were to read. Printed material that only a few years ago would have been puzzling to you gives you no difficulty, or little difficulty, today. And all this time you did not have to consult a dictionary very often to help you in that reading. You seemed to pick up the meanings of words automatically as you went along. The way you usually did that was by unconsciously figuring out what new words must mean from the way they were used, especially as you met those words again and again in different sentences.

This progress would of course continue in college whether you studied this book or not. But this book is designed to help you take a really big step forward. To take that big step you must do several things. ("Must" here means "if you want to get all the help this book is intended to give.") For one, you'll have to pay special attention to

one
an
invitation

certain "big" words that you begin to meet every so often, but which would remain rather vague in meaning if you didn't direct particular attention to them. As a result, this book will send you often to some good desk dictionary, perhaps one recommended by your instructor. That will be one way in which your *study of reading* here will be different from just *reading*—which, of course, you'll continue to do on your own. But you will also, perhaps surprisingly, have to pay attention to the "little words," very little words, that you meet frequently in every book, magazine, or newspaper, but may never have stopped to think about much.

Also, you will acquire the habit of *reading aloud*, and go on from there to the habit of hearing in your mind—even when you are reading silently—the writer's voice. At the moment you may not see the importance of that, nor should you linger here to guess at the way it will help you in understanding what you read. But this book will return to it repeatedly, and gradually make clear to you how and why it is of value.

In addition, you will also step up your natural habit of figuring out the meanings of words from the way they are used. In fact, you will make a systematic study of that process. But you will also push it an important step further by learning to decide on the meaning of whole sentences and in fact whole paragraphs from the sentences and paragraphs surrounding them. Of course this important further step is something you have also been doing for years—especially, for

3

instance, in reading stories. But here you will be improving your reading skill by learning to do it systematically, and in a different kind of reading.

Experienced readers that have had to do a great amount of difficult reading—sometimes about things they are not particularly familiar with or interested in—have found some keys to determine the meaning of sentences or whole paragraphs from the sentences and paragraphs surrounding them. They have found that there are certain devices— tricks, if you like—that they can depend on to help them. You will learn what are probably the best of these devices—the best, and the most easily learned. By observing them in use, and doing exercises in them yourself, you will begin to make them part of your own reading technique. (These devices are mainly ways of following connecting words and recognizing patterns of emphasis—repetition, comparison, contrast, and positioning—which are used to make clear the flow of thought from sentence to sentence and from paragraph to paragraph.)

Besides this work with the meanings of words and with the connection between sentences and paragraphs, there is still a third matter to consider. The kind of reading you are most familiar with may well be the reading of stories, plays, perhaps even poems, descriptions, and articles of information. Articles of information are designed to give you *facts* about something like, say, gold. From an article about gold you might learn all kinds of facts: its use among ancient as well as modern people as money and as jewelry; its rareness as contrasted with metals like iron, copper, even silver; where it can be mined, and how; methods of refining it from its ore; how easily it can be beaten into extremely thin sheets and drawn into very fine wires; how well it conducts electricity, its atomic weight, its solubility; and its worth on the market today. All these facts can be *memorized* and then *repeated*. Indeed, you can memorize most of them in any order you choose. Stop to think about it and you'll see, too, that even rather small children, if given enough time and practice, could memorize them and any other *facts* as well.

But this third kind of reading that we've now finally come to is indeed different. Like an article of information, it may very well give you facts. Some at least of these facts you may need to remember. But its guiding purpose is not to give you *information* but an *explanation* of something. And an explanation has to be, not just memorized, but *understood*. Consider for instance these matters: the use of gold as a monetary standard; bimetallism (the theory that both gold and silver can be used together as a standard); how the supply of gold affects the value of money and vice versa; why American money today has value without a gold backing; why and how the dollar, the pound, the mark, and the lira fluctuate in value. No amount of mere information, no number of mere facts, could enable you to *understand* all that. You could *memorize* somebody else's understanding of it, but that memorization wouldn't make *you* understand.

This third kind of reading matter is intended to give you an *explanation,* that is, a help in *understanding* something like the complicated matter of money, Nietzsche's theory of tragedy, Marx's theory of value, or Freud's theory of latent dream content. All Greek to you now, perhaps, but matters one or more of which you may be called on to understand in college—matters that no mere memorizing of facts will help you with. (When a woman once complained to the eighteenth-century English author and dictionary-maker Samuel Johnson that she could not understand an explanation he had given, he replied: "Madam, I have given you an explanation. An understanding I cannot give you.")

A piece of explanatory prose gives you an explanation, then, but *you* have to do the understanding—by *following* the line of thought that a writer is carrying from paragraph to paragraph through sentence after sentence. This is the third kind of reading I am talking about—the kind that you have had probably the least experience with. It's the hardest kind of reading. And since you've had little experience with it and it's hard, you need some techniques of reading to help you understand it. It's above all these techniques that this book attempts to help you learn.

Only now and then, and only in a simple, unconscious, and unsystematic way, have you used these techniques in the kind of reading you have had to do, or have chosen for yourself. In stories, the plot carries you along. In poems, you have to use other, different techniques. In books and articles of information, all you have had to do is pick up some facts—and often it didn't even matter much in what order those facts were presented, or in what order you learned them.

But now, very differently, you will have to use systematically the techniques you will learn, so that you can start following—from beginning to end—the *line of thought* you will find, for example, in the chapters of a college textbook in economics. This fact is essential to your understanding of what you're doing in this textbook, and why you're doing it. Consider this comparison: following a line of thought in an article of information is like untying a complicated knot. (A *line,* after all, suggests something like a string or rope.) As Aristotle reminds us, the first thing we have to do is *study* the way the knot is put together, by following with our eyes the string or rope as it makes its twists and turns from one end of the knot to the other. If we fail to do that, and go at the thing haphazardly, we are likely to produce only a worse tangle than the one we found at the start. So we follow the knot's twists and turns from beginning to end, untwist and unturn them systematically from beginning to end, and thus untie the knot.

As a second comparison, let me present a bit of arithmetic and ask you to check it:

$$
\begin{array}{r}
123 \\
\times\ 456 \\
\hline
738 \\
615 \\
492 \\
\hline
56088 \\
\end{array}
$$

What did you have to do to check the answer? You began with the first two numbers, checked the individual multiplications—one by one, systematically, in a certain order—and finally checked the addition of the three partial answers in the same way, until you could conclude that the answer was right or wrong. (There is another way to do it: divide 56,088 by 123 to see whether you get 456; or divide it by 456 to see whether you get 123. I invite you to do so, and to notice again the systematic, step-by-step process that you go through.)

Well now, does the reading you have ordinarily done require you to take the same kind of pains as when untying a complicated knot, or working or checking a multiplication? Has it required the learning of step-by-step techniques that long division required you to learn? No, but much of the reading that lies before you will confront you with "knots" and require you to follow a line of thought step by step in order to reach their solution.

Perhaps you don't realize that you have sometimes actually done this careful study, and as a result have come to see something you didn't realize at first was right there for you to see. For instance, when some people hear a popular song for the first time, what they may pay most attention to is the music; they get only a vague idea of what the *words* of the song add up to. But as they take the time to listen to the song repeatedly, they begin to make a great deal of sense out of those lyrics, and to understand them very well—much better than anyone could on just one hearing.

In fact it's not just with words that we gain greater familiarity or skill through repetition and closer and closer attention and study—any pool shark or big winner at poker can tell you that! Think of some hobby or interest of your own, and remember how repeated attention to it made you grow in knowledge and skill. So if in this book we seem to worry a couple of sentences or paragraphs to death, like a dog gnawing a bone, it's because through repeated and careful examination we will find things that we wouldn't otherwise have noticed—things we will need so as to become more skillful readers of difficult material.

"Why, that's a lot of work," you may say. "That isn't *reading* as I've always understood it." Those are exactly my points in this part of my chapter. First, you may have done little if any of this kind of reading. Second, in this kind of reading you may have to take the same kind of trouble—and time—with two sentences as we took in multiplying 123 and 456. And of course you will have to have the same patience in learning the techniques for understanding those two sentences as you once had in learning the techniques of multiplication and division.

Furthermore, because you are learning techniques, you must keep in mind that the selected articles in this book are here *for the sake of your learning those techniques.* You're not learning the techniques so you can read those particular articles. Don't be annoyed if more attention is given to comment and questions than to the articles themselves. Don't be annoyed if the comments and questions "interrupt" the articles. The articles are there only to provide examples of the techniques we have to talk about. But outside this book, and in the articles for reading at the end of the book, you will use the techniques in order to read the material, and not the other way around.

All the same, throughout this book you will of course be interested in *what* the writers you study have to say, if only because of your interest in learning *how to follow* what they say. For instance, suppose a writer studied in this book were to say something like this:

In considering capital punishment, we must stop to think of our idea of a "murderer." Get the picture of him in your mind. He is a criminal type, isn't he? Surly, burly, hulking, menacing in appearance, or sleek and suave but sinister, or perhaps even innocent-looking, but a man whose mind harbors deep, dark thoughts, a man out to "get" people, a ruthless individual who allows nothing to stand in his way. But if we look at the statistics, "he" may in fact be "she." Furthermore, in one case out of ten the murderer is the husband or wife of the victim, may never have committed a crime of any magnitude, and may never commit one again. In fact, if your murderer is not your husband or wife, chances are high that he's the man next door, or a friend down the block, or a person you've been acquainted with for some time—one, perhaps, that you've often spent the evening drinking with down at the corner bar. Or the murderer may be a man or woman you've been romancing, if not indeed some other relative of yours—your brother, sister, mother, father, son, daughter, uncle, cousin, or whatever. Remember, a gun or a knife in the house can be a powerful temptation when, perhaps under the influence of drugs or drinking, someone who has never done anything violent before acts impetuously in a fit of uncontrollable anger. In any case, statistics show that in a large number of cases the murderer may not be our stereotype of a "murderer" at all. You may say, "a person who has murdered once may easily murder again." That's true of the kind of murderer you may have had in mind—the professional hit man, for instance. But unless the person we have been talking about is a homicidally demented individual, or a brawler who has been in trouble with the police before, it does not seem to be true that he or she "may easily murder again."

Another consideration about capital punishment is that it may be serving the murderer's purpose exactly. Some murderers, with a kind of twisted unconscious suicidal impulse, kill someone else so that the state will kill them by means of capital punishment.

For present purposes, the main reason for reading the paragraphs above is not to learn about capital punishment. You will not be asked for your opinion on the subject. Nor will your instructor poll the class, or send you to the library to look for statistics, or bring into class other articles on capital punishment. That would be missing the point altogether. Here we are concerned with entirely different kinds of questions, having to do with exactly what the writer says, how he connects his thoughts, how he handles his argument.

Such questions as these might be asked: Why is capital punishment called *capital*? What is the meaning of the words *hulking, menacing, suave, sinister, ruthless, statistics, magnitude, impetuously, stereotype, homicidally, demented*?

Next, consider the sentence, "He is a criminal type, isn't he?" Is that what the writer thinks, or is it what he imagines you may be thinking? Then look at the description of a murderer that follows. What is it doing in the argument? Is it a picture that the writer wants to present of every kind of murderer? Tell how the statement " 'he' may in fact be 'she' " changes the picture. Does the sentence that begins with "Furthermore" add another point the writer wishes to make, or does it continue the first point? If it's another point, can you see some connection with the first point? How well does the phrase "drinking with down at the corner bar" fit into the general argument? Does the second paragraph continue to make the point of the first paragraph, or does it fit rather into what may be the main idea of the whole article—an article, say, that questions whether capital punishment is desirable? And does the opposite view—one that favors capital punishment—get any representation at all here?

These are the kinds of questions we are interested in as we study the selections in this book. We are trying to learn the general methods used by writers of explanatory articles on *any* subject, and to learn the techniques needed if we are to *cooperate* with those methods and, by that means, *understand* the explanation. Our purpose, therefore, in reading this book is not essentially to acquire information from the articles we read, or to form opinions, or to discuss the ideas encountered. Those things have their place elsewhere. Nor should your instructor simply explain to you what a particular article means, since this assumes that learning the article's message—"Capital punishment is undesirable," for instance—is your goal. Given a problem about "how many shingles will cover a roof ten feet by ten feet, if two shingles cover a space one foot by one foot," a child in an arithmetic class understands that the class is not studying roofing but arithmetic. In the same way, when we looked at the passage just presented, we were studying not capital punishment but reading.

Of course a lively class discussion of capital punishment—or many other topics you can think of—might be much more interesting than a discussion of words, or of relationships between one part of a paragraph and another, or of any other technical matters discussed in this book. But then, *it's always easy to find something more interesting to do than work that ought to be done.*

Finally, let me point out another example that has been right here before your eyes—this chapter itself! It, after all, is an article that attempts to explain something to you. True, I've tried to use only words that freshmen understand—words that they themselves use when they write themes. (Except, of course, in our example of an article on capital punishment.) Also, I've tried to keep most of the sentences reasonably short. All the same, unless you gave it a patient and attentive reading, you may have found that you didn't follow it as well as you could have. So as you glance ahead at the following questions, you may decide to reread the chapter by way of preparation. The questions weren't designed to baffle you. They are simply a little test by which you can prove to yourself that, by reading this chapter, you have understood my point. In fact, maybe they will help you do so.

EXERCISES

1. What is the statement in this chapter that all the rest of the chapter tends to develop—by explaining, giving examples, and so forth? Where is that statement found? Is that where it should be, if it is to guide you in understanding why you are reading the chapter, and what you are reading about? (If this first question turns out to be the hardest of all, ask it of yourself again last.)

2. Does the chapter say you can't read? Explain.

3. The chapter does not say that you ought to read a lot. Does it hint at that anywhere?

4. How do you *usually* learn the meanings of new words you meet in your ordinary reading? What other way is there?

5. You often figure out the meaning of a new word from its use in the sentence. What does the chapter mean when it speaks of pushing that figuring-out an important step further?

6. Why do experienced readers pay particular attention to comparisons and contrasts? What does the chapter indicate as their reason for doing so?

7. *Articles of information* are described in a whole paragraph with a long, detailed example. If they are not the kind of article we are going to be particularly concerned with, why spend so much time on them?

8. Tell in your own words what is meant by an article of explanation.

9. Can you learn facts by merely memorizing them? Why or why not?

10. Can you understand an explanation by merely memorizing it? Why or why not?

11. The chapter spends a lot of time on techniques for reading explanatory prose. What other fairly difficult technique for doing something have you learned earlier during your life? Could you have done that thing without learning the technique? Did you learn the technique yourself, or did someone help you? In either case, who had to do the learning? Could a textbook or an instructor have done it for you? Whether you were on your own or had help, did you do the thing well right away? What was necessary before you were successful?

12. Does this chapter suggest that you will become a skilled reader at once? If not, what does it say?

13. How is a difficult reading passage like a complicated knot?

14. How is reading a difficult paragraph like working a problem in multiplication or long division?

15. For what purpose might you or some other person read an article in a newspaper or magazine that offers a theory about the disappearance of ships and airplanes in the Bermuda triangle?

16. If there were such an article in this book, why would you be asked to read it?

Do not suppose that you are expected to do any more, than your reasonable best to answer these questions, and do not be disappointed if you cannot answer even half of them at this point. If your instructor chooses, or if you yourself wish to, reread this chapter at the end of this course and answer these questions again. You will probably be surprised. You will find this chapter much easier to read and the questions much easier to answer. That will be a highly satisfactory proof to yourself that, at the end of the course, your reading ability has truly improved.

chapter

One day in class an exceptionally able student alluded to a passage she had memorized from Shakespeare. A few other students, it turned out, recalled some parts of it, too. At once I saw in the quotation a chance to show students in a nutshell exactly what their real reading problem is. I can show you the same thing, using the passage she had memorized.

Her quotation was Portia's famous "Mercy" speech from Shakespeare's *Merchant of Venice*. One character in the play, Antonio, has promised in writing to give a pound of his flesh to Shylock, a money-lender, if one of Antonio's friends has not repaid Shylock a sum of money by a certain date. The friend is unable to repay the debt on time, so Antonio must let Shylock cut a pound of flesh from him. He cannot get out of the agreement.

So Portia, pleading in court in defense of Antonio, tries to get him off by arguing that, after all, Shylock has to be merciful. Shylock answers, "On what compulsion must I? Tell me that." Portia responds with her famous "Mercy" speech:

> The quality of mercy is not strained.
> It droppeth as the gentle rain from heaven
> Upon the place beneath. It is twice blest, *etc.*

"Yes," I said, "in my day every young woman knew that speech by heart: 'The quality of mercy is not strained—.' Tell me, what does 'strained' mean here?"

two
the process of reading

My student wondered that I asked the question. Doesn't everybody know what *strained* means? But she answered at some length: *strained* means passed through a strainer—through a sieve, a screen, or whatever. So *not strained* means not limited, not reduced, not partly held back. Along with a few other students, she pointed out that the line "It droppeth as the gentle rain from heaven" shows that Portia means that mercy is free-flowing, not as if passed through a strainer.

I thought this reasoning intelligent, but only in part.

"No," I said, "*strained* can't mean that here."

"Oh yes," my student replied, "I think it does." So far, it was "just the teacher's opinion against the student's," as freshmen sometimes say.

"But," I said, "it's not just a pretty speech about mercy that Shakespeare has dropped into the play. Literature doesn't consist of beautiful pages the writer puts down as they come to him, and that you then admire without quite understanding."

I don't think the students were following me. They wanted me just to get back to why I thought *strained* in Portia's speech could not mean "passed through a strainer," as they thought it obviously did.

"Shylock," I pointed out, "has just demanded an answer. On what compulsion must he be merciful? But before we go on, what does *compulsion* mean?"

A student indicated that it means a compelling, a forcing; that

13

you're compelled—"compulsed," so to speak—if you're made to do something.

"Yes," I said, "and even if a reader doesn't know what *compulsion* means, he does understand *must*. Now Shylock and Portia are debating, and in a debate you can't refuse to pay attention to a question that is part of the debate. So Portia's speech must be an answer to Shylock's question. He asked, why must I be merciful? But to say that "mercy isn't passed through a strainer" would certainly not answer his question; rather it would change the subject, because it's beside the point.

"So," I went on, "Portia's *not strained* has to be an answer to Shylock's 'why must I?' You see, then, *not strained* must mean '*not a must.*' Put the emphasis on the *not* and you'll get the point: 'The quality of mercy is *not* strained'—'not strained' means not compelled, not constrained, not something done on compulsion. We'll have to go into Portia's word 'quality' another time, but 'The quality of mercy is not strained' means that it is of the very nature of mercy that you don't *have* to show it. If you did, it would be justice—to which you *can* compel a person—not mercy. Mercy is freely given. It's like the rain, which you or I can't compel to drop; it just drops."

After hearing my account of that discussion, you may say that, if learning to read better is a process that requires spending all that time on one single word, then it doesn't seem very practical.

My answer is that you should put the emphasis in your question on "process," not on "one single word." My lesson was not on the word *strained,* and its meaning of *constrained* (forced). It was on a process, the process of reading any sentence not just as a little unit by itself, but as the continuation of the thought just preceding. Readers who fail to follow this continuation—that is, to make connections—cannot read well.

Fortunately, this process of continuation, of connection, is something that most readers are capable of doing, and doing well. In my account, the students used this very process in arguing that *not strained* meant "not passed through a strainer," because of the continuation "It droppeth as the gentle rain from heaven." So students *can* do it, but like many readers they haven't been trained to do it *all the time.*

The Merchant of Venice is a play, and therefore a story. And you can follow stories well. Little difficulties like *not strained* won't really rob you of the pleasure of the whole story. But the main business of this book is explanatory prose, not stories. It's nice to be able to read stories, but you don't have to read them. In our society what we all have to read—and understand—is explanatory prose. And when you come to it, difficulties like *not strained* make all the difference! Failure to solve problems like that will rob you of your understanding of a whole article. So it's training in solving puzzles that we must now come to.

First, let's answer some questions.

1. Why did the students think *strained* meant passed through a strainer; in other words, why might you have thought so yourself?

2. Where, according to what I told the students, do we find the clue to what Shakespeare meant by *strained* in that particular line?

3. Explain why what goes before a word more often gives a clue to its meaning than what follows.

4. But can you give an example where something that follows a phrase explains what goes before?

5. Give a simple explanation of how what goes before tells us what the word *steps* means in each of the following pairs of sentences:

   a. Her ballet teacher is teaching her just the five positions in which the feet are held. She is anxious for him to go on to teaching her a few steps.

   b. Now Grandpa has a broken hip. I kept telling you you should have those missing steps repaired.

   c. She thinks she's a big girl now. Last Tuesday she took her first few steps alone.

   d. Making bread from the frozen dough was easy. It involved only a few steps.

   e. The mayor feels that misuse of the park is out of hand. So he plans to take steps.

   f. The old Scotch musical scale had no *fa* in it. So it had just seven steps instead of the usual eight.

   g. Numbers one, two, three, four, five, and six all raise their batons like this. At the same time, number seven steps to the left.

   h. Whenever someone retires, someone else steps into his position at once.

6. Give a simple explanation of why the preceding question about *steps* was easy, whereas the question I asked my student about *strained* was hard.

7. So what, besides looking up words in a dictionary, must we do when we encounter reading material that is rather difficult?

8. The following paragraph may require you to use time, effort, and your dictionary. First, read it as well as you can.

I asked a representative sample of the Berkeley faculty what educational benefits would accrue to the campus as a consequence of our admitting only students "fully prepared in English," as we like to put it. A mathematician was most enthusiastic, explaining that mathematics involves the translation of phenomena into precise language and that precision in the use of the English language is highly correlated with mathematical ability.*

In any difficult reading, the problem is to translate it into your own language. You must (a) use a dictionary as needed; (b) accept help from an instructor or from some textbook when a dictionary fails to help; and especially (c) notice what light the whole of a difficult statement casts on the meanings of the words used in it. In the following discussion we will do all three things.

First, the words likely to be unfamiliar happen to occur at the beginning and end of the passage. As a college student, you surely know the word *faculty*. Now let's go from the known to the unknown. What is "the *Berkeley faculty*"? *Berkeley* is a capitalized word. In some dictionaries you can consult a pronouncing gazetteer (if the capitalized word seems to be a place) or a biographical list of names (if the word seems to name a person). Your dictionary may list two people named Berkeley, at least one of whom might have had a school named after him, but also a *place*. Only certain dictionaries will provide information about the school named Berkeley; most will list it among the colleges and universities that make up still another special section in the back of the dictionary.

Please go through that process yourself, looking up the information even if you knew at once what *the Berkeley faculty* means; this exercise is not a lesson about Berkeley but about the help in reading that a dictionary gives you when you come to *any* capitalized words. Capitalized words are often as important to full understanding as uncapitalized ones.

So, if you've done that work, you can turn now to the first word, *I*. Who is *I*? Since in reading difficult material we need all the help we can get, never neglect to read footnotes (experience tells me most students never read them). *I* is who? Look and see.

*Albert H. Bowker, "Writing Skills and Institutional Articulation," *The Teaching of Expository Writing* (New York: Alfred P. Sloan Foundation, 1978), p. 7.

Now, rather than sending you to the library to consult biographical sources, I will simply tell you that Dr. Bowker, a mathematician and statistician as well as a writer, is the chancellor of the University of California at Berkeley. (Consult your dictionary, if necessary, for *chancellor* and especially for *statistician* and *statistics,* because Dr. Bowker is telling us in this very passage that he used his skill as a statistician to perform his duties as a university chancellor. But look at the title of the book in the footnote, so as to see whether it's only as a mathematician and statistician that Dr. Bowker is being called upon to write.)

Here now is another word that you know: *campus.* But here too the whole passage throws light on what seems to be a familiar word— exactly the point of this lesson, though *all* meanings (vocabulary) are a matter that we can never neglect in any lesson. As used here, does *campus* mean the lawn, trees, benches, or whatever that we think of when we first think of *campus?* Can it even mean people strolling, standing, sitting, or talking on the university lawn? Or have we grasped its meaning if we include in the picture the classrooms and other buildings?

Look at "what educational benefits would accrue to the campus." If you don't know the word *accrue,* try to figure out what it probably means in the sentence, then check that supposed meaning (it should be really *supposed,* not *guessed at*) in your dictionary. Now how could *educational* benefits accrue to lawns and trees? And would Dr. Bowker be interested in educational benefits that accrue only to those who happened to be strolling on the campus? What, then, do you suppose he means by *campus?* Consider: if a father says, "Our house is a happy one" or "Our house is sad today," does he mean the building itself? On the other hand, does Dr. Bowker mean just the English Department? Examine the passage to see whether *campus* doesn't in fact suggest not just the English and perhaps a few other departments, but *every* department.

Next, if you're not sure what *consequence* means here, look it up in your dictionary and then decide which of the meanings that you find there makes sense in Dr. Bowker's sentence. Now, however, comes a real difficulty: Dr. Bowker not only puts "fully prepared in English" within quotation marks, but even adds "as we like to put it." (Be sure you know, or find out, what *put* means in this use.) He says, in other words, that "fully prepared in English" means something particular to the faculty, but could be misunderstood by other people. By students who are "fully prepared in English" he means students so well prepared in reading and writing explanatory material, that no serious problems in reading and writing hold them back in any college classes. (This is not a supposition of mine; it is gathered from his whole article and the whole book containing it.)

Again, Dr. Bowker didn't question every faculty member, as he might have done; he says that he "asked a representative sample of the Berkeley faculty." You had better look up both *representative* and *sample,* even though you know what they mean. Why did he ask just a few? Was it because he wanted to ask only those who would agree with him? Again, what does *representative* mean? (Statisticians are skilled at picking a representative few. A statistician like Dr. George Gallup can come close to predicting how a whole nation will vote by polling not all the bankers, nor all the miners, nor all New Yorkers, but a few people from several main groups that, as experience has shown him, will *represent* the country as a whole.) From these thoughts you perhaps see how *representative* combined with *sample* adds up, in this passage, to a special meaning: Dr. Bowker could tell from the few persons he asked how the whole "campus" would feel.

Now we come to the particular problem with which this lesson began. We've never stopped considering what light one word or expression casts on another, but we began by asking what light one sentence casts on the sentence following it. In the next sentence Dr. Bowker begins, "A mathematician was most enthusiastic." Does the writer mean that the mathematician was an enthusiastic man, or perhaps an enthusiastic professor—the kind whose enthusiastic treatment of triangles or quadratics gets the whole class enthusiastic, too? Or can you link *enthusiastic* with the preceding sentence? For it's not just a question of what *enthusiastic* means—you all know that. It's a question of how *enthusiastic* fits in with what Dr. Bowker is saying. *Enthusiastic* about what? About mathematics? Or—as we're beginning to see—about *what is set forth in the preceding sentence?*

Once you've answered these questions, and explained finally what the chancellor means by his statement, "A mathematician was most enthusiastic," we can turn to an instance of *something following* that throws light on what goes before. But to examine that instance we'll have to look at some individual words. First, *involves.* When you look it up in your dictionary, notice its *etymology*—that is, the Latin *in* and *volv* that it comes from, because from *volv* and its related *volut* we make many words. When you look up *phenomena,* notice that it's a plural, so you may find it under its singular, *phenomenon* (we speak of "two or three phenomena," but "one phenomenon"). Only after you've looked up *phenomenon* can we go on.

Now, out of the meanings your dictionary supplies, which one applies here? Are the phenomena the mathematician is talking about strange, extraordinary facts or events, like the great number of craft disappearing in the Bermuda Triangle? Or are they apples, oranges, triangles, halves, thirds—things we experience every day? Which of these has mathematics dealt with in your classes since as far back as you can remember?

You will have to study the word *correlation* in your dictionary. Statisticians use the word more often than most of us, but not really in a different sense. *High correlation* means "the greater this thing is, the greater that thing is that accompanies it." For example, the more little white aphids you find on a bush, the more ants you're likely to find there, too. That's a high correlation, and a high correlation gives you reason to suspect that there's some *connection* between the aphids and the ants. Is the mathematician then saying that students who write most precisely are *always* those who come with the highest entrance scores in mathematics? No, that would be perfect correlation and would suggest that English and mathematics are essentially the same thing; he just says that there's a high correlation, which suggests that they're much alike (we'll look into this later).

Now, knowing the meanings of the words, we can return to the question, how does what follows the word *enthusiastic* help explain it? To say that these words are all connected is far too general; all parts of a sentence are connected, and every sentence is connected with the one preceding and the one following it. So the question remains, *how* are they connected? Suppose I were to say, "He was enthusiastic. He jumped up and down." Or, "He was enthusiastic, so I felt encouraged." Would these sentences involve a different *kind* of connection from the one I'm asking about? If the question continues to puzzle you, rest assured that we'll come back to that kind of problem later in the book.

When you've finished these questions—orally, in writing, or just by thinking to yourself (depending on what your instructor decides), let's look at the techniques of reading you have learned:

1. In a difficult piece of reading, you probably have to make use of your dictionary, and sometimes every part of it.

2. Your dictionary may give several meanings for a word; you have to select the one that fits, by examining what the rest of the passage is saying. Since there may be more than one unknown word, obliging you to combine unknowns with unknowns, the situation offers something of the same challenge as a jigsaw puzzle.

3. Even when you've chosen the right one among several dictionary definitions, you must at the same time figure out how a writer is using the word here and now. We saw that in the case of *campus* and in the still different case of *enthusiastic*.

4. The only way you can determine what a writer is referring to by

a word he is using here and now, is from seeing how it connects with what has gone before and, in some cases, with what comes after.

Now consider these observations as well:

1. An English assignment in reading can take as much time, work, and thinking as a mathematics assignment. And if, like many students, you have as much difficulty with mathematics as with reading, you know how long that can be!

2. Just as in mathematics, in reading lessons you may have a series of problems all involving one and the same principle. In both subjects you may think you understand the principle, but the problems test whether you really do. Repetition is the mother of learning, and dull though drill may seem, no one has ever found a substitute for it.

3. Clearly—and to demonstrate this, I deliberately chose a difficult passage—some reading assignments are at this point very hard for you, not necessarily because you can't understand them but because, unless they're as short as the passage I gave you from Dr. Bowker, they take more time than you can give them.

4. Nevertheless, even a much easier reading assignment demands, not as much time, but the same kind of hard work, care, and occasional use of the dictionary. By taking that kind of care, you're setting yourself on the road to the more difficult reading you will surely have to do later.

5. This careful work is especially necessary in this book, where you're not just *reading* but *learning to read*. Ask a piano teacher the difference between playing a piece, even several times, and practicing that piece. *Practicing* is what we're doing.

6. You yourself may have read Dr. Bowker's sentences without difficulty and understood them at once. But consider two things: your instructor can hardly use several different texts for the several different levels of reading ability found in most English classes. And more important, if anyway you've generously answered the questions asked, you've understood a process that you too will need when you meet a passage that you yourself find difficult.

7. You probably know the expression, "They can't see the forest for the trees." You can get so deeply involved in the *parts* of what you read, that you miss the continuous flow of thought

that makes the *point* of the whole. After all, the continuous flow of thought is the very principle of this chapter, though it's being applied at present just to individual parts. So turn back and *reread* Dr. Bowker's whole statement so as to get his point. As you know, piano students who endlessly practice individual notes, measures, and passages are not content to do just that; they then play the whole piece. In this book you should *always* reread without interruption any selection whose parts we've stopped to examine. But what you've learned, or will learn, is that the reverse is not necessarily true. When you first read the whole of Dr. Bowker's statement you may, for all I know, have got an idea very different from what your study of the parts revealed as his actual meaning.

chapter

The reading that you probably find difficult is material where a writer tries to explain something to you, tries to get you to follow a line of thought and acquire not only information but *understanding*. To cope with such material, you can use certain techniques. Here we take up an extremely important device by which a writer indicates what his point is and develops his line of thought. In order to get that point and follow that line of thought, we will develop a reading technique that matches this writing device. Our first reading exercise will be an old saying:

Take care of the little things, and the big things will take care of themselves.

This familiar saying may seem to you to involve no reading problem, and thus to offer little or nothing to be learned. But it demonstrates, in a simple and easily understandable way, a basic pattern of expression and therefore a key to understanding.

The pattern to be discovered in that old saying is this: as you go from one part to the other, some elements change and some stay the same. Obviously, *little* changes to *big*, while *take care of* stays the same (in other words, is repeated). A good deal of what you read is based on this simple pattern; the first step in understanding it is just seeing that it's there.

Next, we can go on to *reading the saying aloud*, being careful not to do so as if "reading aloud," but rather as if telling it to someone as in conversation.

three
opposites
attract

If you performed that experiment successfully, you will notice that the emphasis of your voice fell on the words that changed (were opposite, contrasted, opposed), and *not* on the words that stayed the same (were repeated or equivalent). Since that fact is central to our explanation, it bears thinking over: voice emphasis is on things that change, not on things that stay the same. In other words, the oral reading goes like this: "Take care of the LITTLE things, and the BIG things," etc. (There is also emphasis on *themselves,* and for the very reason just given, but to explain that at this point would complicate our discussion.)

If you reversed the emphasis—if you emphasized *take care of* and put no emphasis on *little* and *big*—a person to whom you were talking would probably not understand you and would ask you to repeat the statement. If you think this an exaggeration, try it on an unsuspecting friend, saying perhaps, "DO YOU HAVE YOUR VACATION in winter or DO YOU HAVE YOUR VACATION in summer?" Then see what your friend says.

In other words, we use this emphasis in speech all the time. We always stress what changes over what remains the same, because that's a basic part of English expression. If you remember this as you read aloud, it will help you sound as if you were talking with someone. At the same time, of course, as you learn to read as if talking with someone, you will produce that typical emphasis naturally. Each process will reinforce the other.

But if we do talk with that kind of word stress all the time, and if it is a basic part of English expression, there must be a reason. The reason is that the emphasis and de-emphasis just described are a basic way of *conveying meaning*. If you performed the oral experiment suggested above, you probably discovered that if you reversed the typical emphasis, your hearer didn't get the meaning right away.

This isn't a textbook for an oral interpretation class. Yet the point needs making that the written word developed from the spoken as surely as marching developed from walking. Basically, reading is listening mentally to someone talk. And if readers cannot hear a writer's emphasis—which, as we have seen, is a basic way of conveying meaning—then they cannot be following his line of thought to the point he is striving to make.

So if your instructor chooses to have you read aloud in class, and if you emphasize the elements that change and de-emphasize the elements that remain the same, you will be giving reasonable evidence that you are getting the point. Lacking this evidence in your oral performance, your instructor can hardly judge from it that you are following the line of thought. In any case, reading aloud as part of your homework is essential for improving your reading techniques. And reading aloud is exceptionally important in this chapter, since for most of us emphasis is basically an oral phenomenon, so that we wish to hear what we read.

Next, what about the elements in a piece of writing that stay the same, or are repeated in the same or an equivalent way? Do they play any part in this lesson? They do indeed. It is their function to provide the unchanging background against which the elements that change stand out for us. A simple comparison will make this clear. The page you are looking at right now is all one uniform, unchanging white, and for this reason you can see the capital *t* and the *h* and *e* that begin this sentence. The unchanging white background enables each letter to stand out distinctly as itself, different from all other letters. Similarly, the repetition of *take care of* and *the . . . things* in the saying provides a background that stays the same, so that the words that change—*little* and *big*—can stick out from it.

True, the balance between what changes and what stays the same is less obvious, and probably less important, in a good deal of the writing you read—a kind that you probably don't have much difficulty in following. You will encounter this balance in writing where a writer is trying to *explain* something to you, where you have to follow a line of thought, where you get not only information but understanding. That is the kind of material that is difficult, and for this reason the principle of *different/same*, used so frequently in such material, is of fundamental importance.

EXERCISES

Let's turn now to some exercises that will give you a lively awareness of that principle. First, point out what changes and what remains the same in the following unrelated examples. It's very important that you read each aloud, emphasizing the elements that change while giving no emphasis to the elements that remain the same:

1. God made the country; man made the town.

2. Give me liberty or give me death.

3. A penny saved is a penny earned.

4. In for a penny, in for a pound.

5. Ask not what your country can do for you; ask what you can do for your country.

6. Britain and France had to choose between war and dishonor. They chose dishonor. They will have war. (Note that in the last two of these three sentences there are two pairs of elements that change and must be emphasized.)

7. The most significant thing about the politics of the postwar years was their insignificance. (What contradictions are found here? They must be emphasized.)

8. Love is not love which alters when it alteration finds. (This one is hard.)

9. Everywhere that Mary went the lamb was sure to go.

10. The law of supply and demand proves itself in theory, but sometimes disproves itself in practice.

11. Some people's minds seem better adapted to analyzing things into their parts; other people's minds seem better adapted to synthesizing things into wholes.

12. Are musk roses roses, or are they some other kind of flower?

13. Laugh, and the world laughs with you; cry, and you cry alone.

14. Remember, I'm a Ford and not a Lincoln.

15. Only yesterday, some people were afraid that the United States might be taken over by foreign communists; today, some people are afraid that it is being taken over by foreign capitalists.

16. Some calls me Sarah, some calls me Mary.

17. The age of copper and bronze, of which Egypt had so much, was on its way out, to be superseded by iron, of which Egypt had none.

18. If all American students had been reading nothing but Evelyn Waugh and E. B. White since seventh grade, I am quite sure that they would be writing like angels by the time they got to college.

19. Once people were celebrities because they were important; today they are important because they are celebrities.

20. In order to read well one must not only do a lot of reading, one must do a lot of close reading.

Next comes an exercise not unlike the one you did on the word *steps*. Since you've progressed in your ability to follow a line of thought, you'll find the exercise advanced, but not more difficult.

In the following pairs of sentences, tell which word in the second sentence—always "Today I have something new to tell you"—is to be emphasized, *so as to show its connection with the first*. In the process, you will notice another interesting fact: reading the second sentence with appropriate emphasis will show you how to reread the first sentence so as to give more meaningful emphasis to some element in *it*.

1. Yesterday your father told us the news of his promotion at Sea World. Today I have something new to tell you.

2. Yesterday I thought mistakenly that I had some news for you. Today I have something new to tell you.

3. As usual, yesterday I racked my brains to come up with even a scrap of news. Today I have something new to tell you.

4. You always accuse me of talking about the same old things. Today I have something new to tell you.

5. Usually I just have something new to hear from you. Today I have something new to tell you.

6. It's you who always impart all the hottest items of office gossip to me. Today I have something new to tell you.

Admittedly, if someone else had made up the exercises, I personally would have had some trouble responding to number 3. The word a speaker would emphasize there is *something*. It contrasts with *not even a scrap* and conveys the notion, "it's not much, but it's at least *something*." It's not in the list to be puzzling, though, but to make the list complete. The exercise demonstrates that the sentence "Today I have something new to tell you" has no word in it that *necessarily* receives emphasis. True, if it were standing by itself, a speaker might well give some emphasis to *today* and *new* (for reasons we'll discover later). But in context—as part of a line of thought—it has no word that deserves emphasis except as the sentence contributes to the line of thought.

Here then is something worth thinking over: many a sentence has no word in it that demand emphasis, except as the sentence contributes to the line of thought by having in it an element that *contrasts* with something previously said—or about to be said, as you learned if you went back and read the first of each pair of sentences in the light of the second.

In fact, we can go a step further. Often a sentence (unless standing alone) *has no particular meaning by itself,* and receives its meaning from the context preceding (or in part from the context following). Why can we say that? Because we saw, in earlier experiments in this chapter, that emphasis is a way of conveying meaning. So if there is no particular emphasis, there is no particular meaning. Yet as you study the six pairs of sentences just given, you see clearly that in every case "Today I have something new to tell you" has a very definite meaning—a meaning at least somewhat different in each of the six cases. And you see just as clearly how it received that meaning from the sentence preceding it, just as *steps* did in an earlier exercise. How often, then, in the process of careful, close reading, must we reach back to preceding material to find the meaning of the word, phrase, clause, sentence, or even paragraph that appears before us!

But we learned and practiced that technique of reaching back in an earlier lesson. What new technique have we learned in this lesson? It's the technique of reaching back to some element that is contrasted with a corresponding but different, changed, or new element in what we are now reading. And it's the technique of actually *feeling* the contrast by reading aloud in such a way as to emphasize what changes and de-emphasize what remains the same, or to read silently in such a way as to hear what we read: to hear that same emphasis and de-emphasis that we produce when we read aloud. Finally, we have learned to recognize repeated elements as useful background against which emphatic elements stand out.

We always keep in mind, though, that what we are learning are not tricks of interest in themselves. They are processes that correspond to those processes that the writer himself is using to carry on his line of thought, to make his point, to *explain* something to us in such a way that we acquire not only knowledge but *understanding* from his difficult explanatory prose—the prose that the world of educated people confronts us with.

chapter

To show myself as well as you that "in real life" contraries are used to make a point, I deliberately went to someone *else's* bookcase and picked a book that seemed unpromising. Here is the very first paragraph of Speroni and Golino's textbook *Basic Italian*. Because chosen completely at random, the book and the paragraph itself demonstrate how our newly learned technique of reading can serve us wherever we turn. Except for removing quotation marks around one word, I have changed the text only by printing in italics the words that our technique indicates should receive emphasis. You'll want to read it aloud, carefully stressing the italicized words while sensing that they *are* italicized and stressed, because they're opposites or contrasts, and because it's this opposition that creates the *point*. After the passage you'll find a discussion of what you've just done. Here is the selection:

> This Italian grammar, as its title implies, is a *basic* text and, as such, it is meant to acquaint the student with the *essentials* of Italian grammar. It has been our experience through many years of teaching that in *elementary* courses a *complete* grammar is a *disadvantage* both for the teacher and the student. In our opinion, during the first year the student should learn a *basic* vocabulary and become familiar with the *essential* constructions and patterns of the language. Only after *these* have been properly assimilated can the student go on to the *finer* points of literary style and syntax.*

*Charles Speroni and Carlo L. Golino, *Basic Italian* (New York: Henry Holt and Company, 1958), iii.

four
a matter
of emphasis

As you may have noticed, this whole paragraph contrasts the viewpoint of the authors with an *opposite* viewpoint—which, though not expressed, is clearly understood. How would you express that opposite viewpoint? Would it be fair to say that our authors have in mind, and are opposed to, an older style of first-year Italian grammar that required students to learn a good many Italian words, including rare ones found only in fine literature, along with a number of rules—and exceptions—that are not much needed in simple Italian?

Why is *basic* italicized? What is it being opposed to? Not to anything expressed (at least, not until the last half of the sentence that ends the paragraph), but to something immediately clear all the same. And why is *essentials* italicized? What is its opposite—which we're evidently *not* going to find in this textbook? Why is *elementary* italicized? For what courses would a *complete* grammar be an *advantage*? Would it be fair to say that the contrast our authors have in mind is this: "In advanced courses a complete grammar would be an advantage; but in a beginners' course the whole of Italian grammar would be as much a hindrance as a help." Do the italics, then, seem to make sense—to make the point—as you find them here: "In *elementary* courses a *complete* grammar is a *disadvantage*"?

Next, to what are our authors contrasting *basic* and *essential*? If they are contrasting these words with something, they ought to be italicized here, and as you read the sentence containing them aloud—or hear it in your head as you read silently—you will find that emphasizing them makes sense.

In the last sentence the two elements being contrasted are both expressed. What are they? Are they italicized? As you read the sentence aloud, does a heavy emphasis on *these* and *finer* seem to make sense? As you hear what you read—as you read the sentence silently and *hear* these two words emphasized in your mind—do you find them making the same good sense?

But, someone may say, *any* word in the paragraph can be assumed to be a contrast with something else, in which case you would have to italicize and emphasize it. Yes, Italian *grammar* could form a contrast with Italian *guidebook* or Italian *cookbook*. But could anyone pretend that such a contrast is meant? Once one got the idea that our authors were contrasting their book with a guidebook or a cookbook, would the rest of the paragraph make sense? I think you see that the emphases we have indicated are valid—and that is precisely the point.

On the other hand, there certainly are other words that could be emphasized for the very same reason as the words we have indicated. To find them would require some thought, as with them the implied contrast is more subtle and therefore less necessary. In this course we are concerned with basics; only after these have been properly assimilated, should one go on to the finer points of emphasis. (Sound familiar?) But it won't hurt to look at a few of these other words, just to see the possibilities. First, "*This* Italian grammar" in contrast with others, say the old one by Grandgent. "It has been *our* experience." In contrast with whose? Possibly those who have not had the authors' "many years of teaching." Then, "In *our* opinion." We gather that they know of or can imagine others having a contrary opinion—again, maybe someone teaching Italian to beginners for the first time. "*Properly assimilated*": is there a hint here that if you overload beginners' minds with "the finer points of literary style and syntax," they won't get a secure grasp on the basics—without which, of course, the "finer points" would be senseless? No, it won't hurt you to look at these subtler contrasts, though they are not our concern at present. For now, it's enough if, seeing "wet" in one sentence and "dry" in another, you realize that they form a contrast and that this contrast is making the point; you will then emphasize these two words in order to spotlight them, thus showing that you are solidly aware of the point being made.

Finally, here are three selections to practice on without detailed help from this book. You will certainly want to read each aloud so as to hear yourself emphasizing words or expressions that state or imply a contrast of any kind. These selections, unlike the one that began this chapter, were not chosen at random. They are well known, and well known for the contrasts they present. You may find them increasingly difficult, however. But except for directing your attention to the word *any* near the beginning of the Gettysburg Address, and asking you to ask yourself with whom "we" are being contrasted in that address, I will leave you on you own.

from A TALE OF TWO CITIES, Chapter 1
Charles Dickens

It was the best of times, it was the worst of times, it was the age of wisdom, it was the age of foolishness, it was the epoch of belief, it was the epoch of incredulity, it was the season of Light, it was the season of Darkness, it was the spring of hope, it was the winter of despair, we had everything before us, we had nothing before us, we were all going direct to Heaven, we were all going direct the other way—in short, the period was so far like the present period that some of its noisiest authorities insisted on its being received, for good or for evil, in the superlative degree of comparison only.

THE GETTYSBURG ADDRESS
Abraham Lincoln

November 19, 1863

Four score and seven years ago our fathers brought forth on this continent, a new nation, conceived in Liberty, and dedicated to the proposition that all men are created equal.

Now we are engaged in a great civil war, testing whether that nation or any nation so conceived and so dedicated, can long endure. We are met on a great battle-field of that war. We have come to dedicate a portion of that field, as a final resting place for those who here gave their lives that that nation might live. It is altogether fitting and proper that we should do this.

But, in a larger sense, we can not dedicate—we can not consecrate—we can not hallow—this ground. The brave men, living and dead, who struggled here, have consecrated it, far above our poor power to add or detract. The world will little note, nor long remember what we say here, but it can never forget what they did here. It is for us the living, rather, to be dedicated here to the unfinished work which they who fought here have thus far so nobly advanced. It is rather for us to be here dedicated to the great task remaining before us—that from these honored dead we take increased devotion to that cause for which they gave the last full measure of devotion—that we here highly resolve that these dead shall not have died in vain—that this nation, under God, shall have a new birth of freedom—and that government of the people, by the people, for the people, shall not perish from the earth.

INAUGURAL ADDRESS
John F. Kennedy

January 20, 1961

We observe today not a victory of party but a celebration of freedom—symbolizing an end as well as a beginning—signifying renewal as well as change. For I have sworn before you and Almighty God the same solemn oath our forebears prescribed nearly a century and three-quarters ago.

The world is very different now. For man holds in his mortal hands the power to abolish all forms of human poverty and all forms of human life. And yet the same revolutionary beliefs for which our forebears fought are still at issue around the globe—the belief that the rights of man come not from the generosity of the state but from the hand of God.

We dare not forget today that we are the heirs of that first revolution. Let the word go forth from this time and place, to friend and foe alike, that the torch has been passed to a new generation of Americans—born in this century, tempered by war, disciplined by a hard and bitter peace, proud of our ancient heritage—and unwilling to witness or permit the slow undoing of those human rights to which this nation has always been committed, and to which we are committed today at home and around the world.

Let every nation know, whether it wishes us well or ill, that we shall pay any price, bear any burden, meet any hardship, support any friend, oppose any foe to assure the survival and the success of liberty.

This much we pledge—and more.

To those old allies whose cultural and spiritual origins we share, we pledge the loyalty of faithful friends. United, there is little we cannot do in a host of co-operative ventures. Divided, there is little we can do—for we dare not meet a powerful challenge at odds and split asunder.

To those new states whom we welcome to the ranks of the free, we pledge our word that one form of colonial control shall not have passed away merely to be replaced by a far more iron tyranny. We shall not always expect to find them supporting our view. But we shall always hope to find them strongly supporting their own freedom—and to remember that, in the past, those who foolishly sought power by riding the back of the tiger ended up inside.

To those people in the huts and villages of half the globe struggling to break the bonds of mass misery, we pledge our best efforts to help them help themselves, for whatever period is required—not because the Communists may be doing it, not because we seek their votes, but because it is right. If a free society cannot help the many who are poor, it cannot save the few who are rich.

To our sister republics south of our border we offer a special pledge—to convert our good words into good deeds—in a new alliance for progress—to assist free men and free governments in casting off the chains of poverty. But this peaceful revolution of hope cannot become the prey of hostile powers.

Let all our neighbors know that we shall join with them to oppose aggression or subversion anywhere in the Americas. And let every other power know that this hemisphere intends to remain the master of its own house.

To that world assembly of sovereign states, the United Nations, our last best hope in an age where the instruments of war have far outpaced the instruments of peace, we renew our pledge of support—to prevent it from becoming merely a forum for invective—to strengthen its shield of the new and the weak—and to enlarge the area in which its writ may run.

Finally, to those nations who would make themselves our adversary, we offer not a pledge but a request: that both sides begin anew the quest for peace, before the dark powers of destruction unleashed by science engulf all humanity in planned or accidental self-destruction.

We dare not tempt them with weakness. For only when our arms are sufficient beyond doubt can we be certain beyond doubt that they will never be employed.

But neither can two great and powerful groups of nations take comfort from our present course—both sides overburdened by the cost of modern weapons, both rightly alarmed by the steady spread of the deadly atom, yet both racing to alter that uncertain balance of terror that stays the hand of mankind's final war.

So let us begin anew—remembering on both sides that civility is not a sign of weakness, and sincerity is always subject to proof. Let us never negotiate out of fear. But let us never fear to negotiate.

Let both sides explore what problems unite us instead of belaboring those problems which divide us.

Let both sides, for the first time, formulate serious and precise proposals for the inspection and control of arms—and bring the absolute power to destroy other nations under the absolute control of all nations.

Let both sides seek to invoke the wonders of science instead of its terrors. Together let us explore the stars, conquer the deserts, eradicate disease, tap the ocean depths, and encourage the arts and commerce.

Let both sides unite to heed in all corners of the earth the command of Isaiah—to "undo the heavy burdens . . . [and] let the oppressed go free."

And if a beachhead of co-operation may push back the jungle of suspicion, let both sides join in creating a new endeavor, not a new balance of power, but a new world of law, where the strong are just and the weak secure and the peace preserved.

All this will not be finished in the first one hundred days. Nor will it be finished in the first one thousand days, nor in the life of this administration, nor even perhaps in our lifetime on this planet. But let us begin.

In your hands, my fellow citizens, more than mine, will rest the final success or failure of our course. Since this country was founded, each generation of Americans has been summoned to give testimony to its national loyalty. The graves of young Americans who answered the call to service surround the globe.

Now the trumpet summons us again—not as a call to bear arms, though arms we need—not as a call to battle, though embattled we are—but a call to bear the burden of a long twilight struggle, year in and year out, "rejoicing in hope, patient in tribulation"—a struggle against the common enemies of man: tyranny, poverty, disease, and war itself.

Can we forge against these enemies a grand and global alliance, North and South, East and West, that can assure a more fruitful life for all mankind? Will you join in that historic effort?

In the long history of the world, only a few generations have been granted the role of defending freedom in its hour of maximum danger. I do not shrink from this responsibility—I welcome it. I do not believe that any of us would exchange places with any other people or any other generation. The energy, the faith, the devotion which we bring to this endeavor will light our country and all who serve it—and the glow from that fire can truly light the world.

And so, my fellow Americans: ask not what your country can do for you—ask what you can do for your country.

My fellow citizens of the world: ask not what America will do for you, but what together we can do for the freedom of man.

Finally, whether you are citizens of America or citizens of the world, ask of us here the same high standards of strength and sacrifice which we ask of you. With a good conscience our only sure reward, with history the final judge of our deeds, let us go forth to lead the land we love, asking His blessing and His help, but knowing that here on earth God's work must truly be our own.

chapter

You must continue to make yourself aware of the accent that falls on *contrasted* words in a sentence or in adjoining sentences. Look for examples in the reading you have to do for other purposes, and when you find them, read the sentence aloud (or in your mind pretend to read it aloud), always with the natural stress: "In GOD we TRUST; all OTHERS pay CASH." "SPEECH is SILVER: SILENCE is GOLDEN." (Try emphasizing, instead, the two *is*'s in that sentence, and see what happens!) Remember that you always get the accent right when you talk to your friends and family, so read every sentence as if you were telling it to someone. Read it that way even when reading to yourself silently, for we must always listen to what we read.

But besides this accent (stress, emphasis) on words or phrases that change or are contrasted, there are other kinds of accent, equally important for understanding, that we must examine in this chapter. Let me approach the matter by saying that some students, when I call on them individually to read a sentence aloud in class, read in such a weak voice that they can hardly be heard. I find that, by straining, usually I can hear all of the sentence *except the last word or phrase.*

What does that indicate? It indicates so many things that I scarcely know where to begin. Let me explain first what these students are actually doing: they are swallowing—which is the same as *omitting*—the very point of the sentence! Why do I say that? Because the rule—a rule people usually follow automatically when they talk—is that in our sentences we put our point *at the end.*

five
happy
endings

Let us demonstrate this. Using your technique of reaching back to preceding context for the meaning of a sentence you're reading, you will easily see, in the second of each of the following pairs of sentences, what the point is, and you will note that the point is at the end. (In reading the sentences aloud, if you emphasize the end, you will notice that the emphasis sounds "right.")

> I believed I had passed his little test. After some careful thinking, I had answered his three questions.

What's the point? Why did I think I had passed his test? Because I had *answered his questions*. And that comes at the end. How different it would be if our sentence went like this:

> I knew she didn't want me to give any careless answers. So I answered her three questions after some careful thinking.

Now what's the point? If I'm not to give a careless answer, what do I have to do? And where do I say that I do it? So "after some careful thinking" changes position according to whether it is, or is not, the point.

Now let's look carefully at another pair of sentences, because they are going to lead us on to another valuable technique in reading:

> I was talking with a bookseller about printing type faces, and said I wondered where I could find a good library of typography. He told me I would probably have to go to Chicago.

Now—besides noting that the second sentence would be a mystery without the first—ask yourself with what one little word in the first sentence the word *Chicago* in the second corresponds. Has the bookseller caught the point of my first sentence? Has he met that point with a corresponding point in the second? And where has he put his point?

In this example, on close inspection you find that the second sentence has actually answered a question in the first: Where can I find such a library? Chicago. Writers sometimes test their way of constructing a sentence by pretending their sentence is an answer to a question. "If this were an answer to a question," they ask themselves, "what would that question be?" Suppose I write this sentence: "Bees finding a blossom too long and narrow for the nectar to be reached, will quickly puncture a petal through its base in many instances." But then I ask myself whether I want to answer the imagined question, "How often do bees do that?" or the question, "what do bees, in the case described, do?" Actually, I've answered the first, because I've put "in many cases" at the end. If instead I want to answer the second, I've got to remove "in many instances" from the end by either tucking it inside the sentence or at least putting it at the beginning: "In many instances, bees finding a blossom too long and narrow for the nectar to be reached, will quickly puncture a petal through its base."

Of course this is only one device whereby writers ask themselves, "What's my point?" (Another way would be to ask themselves, "Could I conceivably *underline* what I've got at the end?" If they can't, what they have there doesn't belong there.)

You can judge the importance of this technique—or whatever substitutes for it—when I tell you that a writer whose work I admire highly gives me his work to check over, and that almost the only fault I ever find with it is that sometimes he has failed to ask himself, "What question would my sentence answer?" As a result, he puts something wrong at the end.

Now if writers can use that technique in *indicating* their point, we can get practice in *finding* their point by using the same technique. As I've intimated, there are other techniques that accomplish the same purpose. But because of my experience with students, this is the one I have chosen. So we are going to use this technique—artificial though it may seem, and a little hard to catch on to at first—to illustrate what I was saying earlier: that people in ordinary conversation communicate their point to us by putting it *at the end*. Now we are going to test this rule, and gain familiarity with it, by imagining what question a statement would answer and noticing that the answer—the point—comes at the end.

Thus, for instance, the sentence "Today I'm going to clean my cupboards" answers the question, "What are you going to do today?" (At this point the matter becomes a little complicated, because in a question the point, or key expression, usually comes not last but first. This complication, however, need not hold us up.)

If the question is "What are you going to do today?" the key point of the answer is clearly "clean my cupboards." In fact, the answer could actually be shortened to that: "What are you going to do today?" "Clean my cupboards." (Certainly the answer could not be "today" or "I'm going to.")

But suppose we change the question to "When are you going to clean your cupboards?" You would be unlikely to answer that question by saying, "Today I'm going to clean my cupboards." To clearly communicate the time, "today" is in the wrong place. Since "today" is the key answer to "when?" you would put it where the key—the point—belongs: at the end. "When are you going to clean your cupboards?" "I'm going to clean them today."

Mind you, there's more in this analysis than meets the eye. Here as elsewhere, I hope to teach you some things about reading without your being aware of what I'm doing. But here I do want you to be aware of this: that the point of a sentence is usually at the end, so when reading aloud you must increase your volume and stress, so that the end of each sentence rings out loud and clear.

"But," you may say, "surely this isn't a book to train us to read aloud?" No, it isn't. But if students, in reading aloud, swallow the end of a sentence, certainly they can't be very conscious of the fact that they have swallowed—virtually omitted—the point. And this suggests that they cannot be very conscious of what the point is meant to be. You may of course answer that reading a sentence aloud is such an effort, that by the end the exhausted students can only mutter. But I would still insist that if they realized keenly that the sense is typically at the end, they would make a supreme effort to deliver the sentence's message—its end—loud and clear (and then, like the wounded drummer boy who delivered the news of victory to Napoleon, smile as they fall dead).

Of course there's more to all this than that. The basic reason why students don't realize that the point of a sentence ordinarily comes at the end, is that they are not aware that a sentence *has* a point. It is, for them, an item of information listed with some other items of information—other sentences—on a page. That is, a page to them is something like a grocery list, where *understanding* is not the issue. What they must come to see is that a page of explanatory prose is not like a grocery list, but like a geometry proposition, where the point of any sentence takes its meaning from the preceding sentence and adds to that meaning. Obtaining a keen awareness of this *line of reasoning* in sentences is a slow, step-by-step process; the matters of emphasis treated in this and the preceding chapter are two of the necessary steps.

EXERCISES

Now let's get some practice in seeing the point of the ordinary sentence at the end. In the following unrelated practice sentences, which I beg you to read aloud, I will put the point in italics.

1. Tomorrow, the governor is going to have *a terrible awakening.* (*What* is the governor going to have?)

2. The story you told me yesterday was *a lie.* (*What* was the story you told me yesterday?)

3. My birthday is *Monday.* (*When* is your birthday?)

4. Monday is *my birthday.* (*What* is Monday?)

5. God helps those *who help themselves.* (*Which people* does God help?)

6. Yet students should also notice that the point the author is seeking to make is actually *the converse.* (*What* should they notice that his point is?)

7. True, this balance between what changes and what stays the same is less obvious, and less important, *in a good deal of the writing you'll encounter.* (*Where* is the balance less obvious?)

8. True, in most of the writing you'll encounter, this balance between what changes and what stays the same is *less obvious and less important.* (*What* is the balance there like?)

9. Lawes *set Waller's poem to music.* (*What* did Lawes do?)

10. Waller's "Go, Lovely Rose" was set to music *by Lawes.* (*Who* set Waller's poem to music?)

Now in the following examples the italics—and the question that each sentence answers—must be supplied mentally, or better still vocally, by you.

1. But the truth is that they show, in a simple and understandable way, a basic pattern of expression.

2. People in some parts of Ireland, whose ancestors spoke a language—Gaelic—that showed every emphasis so readily by the position of every word in a sentence, speak English in an unemphatic monotone. (Please note: The writer says that those people "speak English." Is the fact that they "speak English" the point of his sentence? What point is he making? How does his sentence show what his point is?)

3. Far from speaking in a monotone, other Irish speakers, keenly aware—as a heritage from Gaelic—of the importance of emphasis, speak English in a very lively and emphatic fashion.

4. Throwing Latin out of high schools placed a staggering burden on English classes.

5. For thus the grammatical and syntactical analysis which was routine in Latin classes had now to be done in English classes. (Look up in a dictionary *grammar, grammatical, syntax, syntactical, analysis, analytical, synthesis, synthetic, routine* as an adjective, and *thus.*)

6. By sitting in a chilly room in his shirtsleeves, he caught cold.

7. He caught cold by sitting in a chilly room in his shirtsleeves.

8. The mother of learning is frequent repetition.

9. Frequent repetition is the mother of learning.

10. Only one danger is that you may break the glass.

11. That you may break the glass is only one danger.

12. Early in the century the saxophone was treated as a serious instrument. (How do we know what's to be emphasized— what the point is? What would be the opposite of that point?)

13. The saxophone was treated as a serious instrument earlier in the century. (The point is that it's not treated seriously any more, but that it was so earlier.)

What, you may ask, am I to do when (a) there's a contrast, and (b) neither of the words or expressions contrasted—and therefore to be emphasized—comes at the end? Am I still to emphasize the end? No, certainly not if at the end there comes an element that stays the same. Consider this example: "You take the top of it, and I'll take the bottom of it." Of course you are to emphasize *you* and *I, top* and *bottom,* and certainly not *of it* at the end of either clause.

Similarly, what about "Don't change horses in the middle of the stream"? Are you to emphasize "the stream"? No, that wouldn't make sense. The saying "Don't change horses in the middle of the stream" urges you not to make changes in some activity that's incomplete, so the key word is *middle.* "Don't change horses in the middle." But naturally one asks, "Middle of what?" So you emphasize the whole ending, *middle of the stream.* (The idea, of course, is that if you make some change midway, you may come to grief, just as a horseman who changes mounts while fording or swimming a river may get wet or even drown.)

But "Don't change horses in the middle of the stream" may make us notice something else. Normally, the most important part of a sentence or clause—the part that contains the *point*—is the end, which therefore normally deserves the greatest emphasis. But the second most important point of a sentence or clause is the beginning, which therefore deserves some emphasis, too. At least it does if you can see that the writer has put some part of his point there.

But you'll probably want to direct attention—*your* attention, which is what's important—to those beginning words or expressions, not by the kind of emphasis you're giving either to the ends of sentences or to contrasting elements anywhere in sentences, but by some other means: (a) by pausing briefly after them, or (b) by giving them a little higher musical pitch, or (c) by saying them a little more slowly than what follows them. It doesn't matter how you do it, so don't get hung up on trying to find the "right" way. Just do whatever comes natural to you, in order to direct somewhat special attention to those beginnings.

Now read the following exercises aloud, emphasizing (a) the end of each, or (b) any contrasted elements, just as before; but at the same time pause a little after (c) the beginning (or whatever you want to do to give that beginning some emphasis).

1. Necessity is the mother of invention.

2. July 14 is celebrated in France as Bastille Day.

3. Time heals all wounds.

4. Into everyone's life some rain must fall. (The first three words are the beginning; all the rest is the ending. Give additional stress to *everyone's,* because it's an implied contrast to "not just some people's." You may also want to stress *some,* with its implied contrast to "You can't expect *no* rain." Practice sentence 4 three or four times.)

5. Josephus wrote a history of the Jews.

6. Beethoven wrote the Moonlight Sonata.

7. Milton wrote *Paradise Lost.*

8. When clouds mass in the southwest, we may have a tornado. (Notice that the writer's point might be represented thus: "clouds—southwest—tornado." That gives you an idea of what words to emphasize.)

9. The great enemy of clear language is insincerity.

10. The only purpose for which power can be rightfully exercised over any member of a civilized community, against his will, is to prevent harm to others.

11. It was the best of times; it was the worst of times.

12. Learning something is the greatest of pleasures, not just for the thinker, but for all other men too, even those who can learn very little. (First read that three or four times, then answer this: in this statement by Aristotle, do you find elements that ought to be emphasized, even though they are not of the kinds we have discussed—that is, not opposites, endings, or beginnings? Good. Why do you think they should be emphasized? If you didn't find any, consider *greatest, not just, all, too, even,* and *very.* In what way that would justify their being emphasized are these expressions alike?)

13. Although she couldn't drive a car, and although the colleges she had to attend were quite distant, she managed year after year to arrange transportation and got both her B.A. and her M.A.

Notice that this last sentence contains not one statement—called a clause—but several: The first begins with *although,* the second with *and although,* and the last with *she managed,* while *she had to attend* is a clause within the clause "the colleges . . . were quite distant." Moreover, both *to arrange* and *got* can be thought of as beginning separate statements. Now go back to the sentence and see for yourself if what I've just said is so. My point in directing your attention to these clauses is this: in applying the proper emphasis, one must treat each clause as if it were a separate sentence. Accordingly, you'll emphasize *drive a car,* then *quite distant* (with a slighter emphasis on *the colleges*), then *transportation* (with a slighter emphasis on *managed*), then *B.A.* and—strongest emphasis of all—*M.A.*

Finally, I want you to go back and study, practice, and drill on that same thirteenth exercise and the explanation that follows it. I realize that repeating an exercise over and over (drilling) isn't very entertaining; but in order to read profitably for the rest of your life, you must form the habit of catching the full point of what you are reading by noting the meaningful—and meaning-conveying—emphases. And the only way to form a habit is by repetition.

In fact, if I were your instructor, I would have all of you read the exercises aloud in class. I would stay on these first chapters until I was sure you got the point and were reading with satisfactory emphasis.

So drill on that last sentence—giving attention to the explanation that follows it—until you know for certain that you see clearly the point of what you are doing, and know that you are doing it well.

In concluding with a passage from Eric Ambler's novel *A Coffin for Dimitrios* (you may wish to read the whole book someday), you will notice that—except for a colloquial touch here and there like "you know"—every sentence ends ringingly on the point. Years ago I myself used to read it aloud for practice. What is your experience in reading it aloud?

YOU SEE THE IDEA
Eric Ambler

Eric Ambler is an English writer who specializes in novels of foreign intrigue. He has also written and produced several films.

Then Mr. Peters took a cigarette, wetted the end of it with his tongue and lit it.

"Have you ever known a drug addict, Mr. Latimer?" he asked suddenly.

"I don't think so."

"Ah, you don't *think* so. You do not know for certain. Yes, it is possible for a drug-taker to conceal his little weakness for quite a time. But he—and especially *she*—cannot conceal it indefinitely, you know. The process is always roughly the same. It begins as an experiment. Half a gramme, perhaps, is taken through the nostrils. It may make you feel sick the first time; but you will try again and the next time it will be as it should be. A delicious sensation, warm, brilliant. Time stands still; but the mind moves at a tremendous pace and, it seems to you, with incredible efficiency. You were stupid; you become highly intelligent. You were unhappy; you become carefree. What you do not like you forget; and what you do like you experience with an intensity of pleasure undreamed of. Three hours of Paradise. And afterwards it is not too bad; not nearly as bad as it was when you had too much champagne. You want to be quiet; you feel a little ill at ease; that is all. Soon you are yourself again.

Nothing has happened to you except that you have enjoyed yourself amazingly. If you do not wish to take the drug again, you tell yourself you need not do so. As an intelligent person you are superior to the stuff. Then, therefore, there is no logical reason why you should not enjoy yourself again, is there? Of course there isn't! And so you do. But this time it is a little disappointing. Your half a gramme was not quite enough. Disappointment must be dealt with. You must wander in Paradise just once more before you decide not to take the stuff again. A trifle more; nearly a gramme perhaps. Paradise again and still you don't feel any the worse for it. And since you don't feel any the worse for it, why not continue? Everybody knows that the stuff does ultimately have a bad effect on you; but the moment you detect any bad effects *you* will stop. Only fools become addicts. One and a half grammes. It really is something to look forward to in life. Only three months ago everything was so dreary; but now . . . Two grammes. Naturally, as you are taking a little more it is only reasonable to expect to feel a little ill and depressed afterwards. It's four months now. You must stop soon. Two and a half grammes. Your nose and throat get so dry these days. Other people seem to get on your nerves, too. Perhaps it is because you are sleeping so badly. They make too much noise. They talk so loudly. And what are they saying? Yes, *what?* Things about *you,* vicious lies. You can see it in their faces. Three grammes. And there are other things to be considered; other dangers. You have to be careful. Food tastes horrible. You cannot remember things that you have to do; important things. Even if you should happen to remember them, there are so many other things to worry you apart from this beastliness of having to live. For instance, your nose keeps running: that is, it is not really running but you think it must be, so you have to keep touching it to make sure. Another thing: there is always a fly annoying you. This terrible fly never *will* leave you alone and in peace. It is on your face, on your hand, on your neck. You must pull yourself together. Three and a half grammes. You see the idea, Mr. Latimer?"

chapter

In a previous lesson we read a sentence that mentioned the high correlation between skills in English and skills in mathematics. Personally, I would rather emphasize simply the sequential method that mathematics teachers find successful, and the need for the same kind of patient analytical work in reading as is required in even long division. However, reading and mathematics do bear enough resemblance that it may be useful for those of you concerned with mathematics to consider that a piece of explanatory prose has a flow of thought from line to line somewhat like an algebra problem that has been worked out, or a geometry proposition. The practical question for you mathematicians is, can you carry over into your reading the kind of step-by-step thinking you do in mathematics? Can you make the "transfer," as we like to put it?

Having often been a foreign-language teacher, I see an even closer correlation between learning to read English and learning to read a foreign language. If you have studied a foreign language you know how, upon meeting a sentence you can't read, sooner or later you must look up the unknown words in a dictionary or word list, and sometimes have to juggle the several meanings you find till you figure out the right one for each word. (I'll never forget the trouble I once had with the German expression *zum Zuge kommen* in a translation I had to make hurriedly for a certain department of the government. The expression could mean "to come to the train," but that meaning didn't make any

six
slowly
does it

sense in the context—the particular passage—I was translating. The only dictionary I had was of no help. Finally a native German came to my aid: *zum Zuge kommen* also means to get one's turn—in chess, checkers, or whatever. And this meaning fit perfectly in the context: "Now it's China's turn" made sense there, whereas "Now China comes to the train" was nonsense.)

The practical point is this: average students who for some time have been taking Spanish, Latin, or another foreign language, come to the few assigned pages for the next day's lesson prepared to look up several words and to figure out carefully how those words are put together to make sense. Now the written English you meet in moderately difficult articles by professional writers is to a certain extent *a foreign language* for you. You have the same problems of looking up words and of figuring out how those words fit together to make sense.

To sum up: in the United States many college freshmen have trouble doing the kind of reading required in college classes and afterward. They can make a substantial start in overcoming that problem if, in the freshman year, they submit to the same kind of step-by-step method and the same kind of exacting, patient work, including repetitive drill, that is done in mathematics, piano, and foreign languages.

Instructors countrywide tell me that occasionally a student asks them about speed reading. Speed reading—which fifty years ago was called skimming—is the obvious answer when what you have to read is much too long for the time at your disposal (it's either skim it or not read it at all), or when it's not much worth reading anyway (like an advertisement in the mail for black lingerie or for power tools you don't need anyway), or when it lies outside your field of understanding (like the figures in an annual report of a company in which your family are shareholders). But just as obviously, a person who wants to read Shakespeare's *Hamlet* in twenty minutes or the Bible in two hours is missing the whole point of *Hamlet* and the Bible. For that would be like wanting to see all of Disneyland and complete all its rides in ten minutes, or to rewatch your favorite motion picture or TV show condensed to five minutes in length.

Still, in the real world do people—practical, successful, able people—do any of the slow reading that this book has been calling on you to do? If so, do they do it just for pleasure, or do they feel there are practical benefits from it? Perhaps the following selection—which in itself is lively reading—will suggest a thoughtful answer to these questions.

THE SPECIAL JOYS OF SUPER-SLOW READING
Sidney Piddington

Sidney Piddington is an advertising executive in Sydney, Australia.

Even for the pressure-cooker world of advertising, it had been a frustrating, tension-building day. I took home a briefcase full of troubles. A major contract was in danger of being lost at the last minute, two executives of a company with whom we hoped to clinch a deal were being elusive, and a strike threatened the opening of a business that held my money and my future.

As I sat down on that hot and humid evening, there seemed to be no solutions to the problems thrashing around in my brain. So I picked up a book, settled into a comfortable chair and applied my own special therapy—super-slow reading.

I spent three hours on two short chapters of *Personal History* by Vincent Sheean—savoring each paragraph, lingering over a sentence, a phrase, or even a single word, building a detailed mental picture of the scene. No longer was I in Sydney, Australia, on a sticky heat-wave night. Relishing every word, I joined foreign correspondent Sheean on a mission to China and another to Russia. I lost myself in the author's world, *living* his book. And when finally I put it down, my mind was totally refreshed.

Next morning, four words from the book—"take the long view"—were still in my mind. At my desk, I had a long-view look at my problems. I concluded that the strike would end sooner or later, so I made positive plans about what to do then. The two executives would see me eventually; if not, I would find other customers. That left me free to concentrate on the main thing, saving the contract. Once more, super-slow reading had given me not only pleasure but perspective, and helped me in my everyday affairs.

I discovered its worth years ago, in the infamous Changi prison-of-war camp in Singapore. I was nineteen, an artillery sergeant, when the city fell to the Japanese on February 15, 1942. Waiting with other Australian POWs to be marched off, I tried to decide what I should take in the single pack permitted. The only limit was what a weary man could carry the seventeen miles to Changi. Our officer thoughtfully suggested, "Each man should find room for a book."

So I stuffed into my pack a copy of Lin Yutang's *The Importance of Living*—a title of almost macabre appropriateness—and began a reading habit that was to keep me sane for the next three and a half years. Previously, if I had been really interested in a book, I would race from page to page, eager to know what came next. Now, I decided, I had to become a miser with words and stretch every sentence like a poor man spending his last dollar.

During the first few days at Changi, I took Lin Yutang out of my pack three or four times, just gazing at the cover, the binding and the illustrated inside cover. Finally, as the sun went down one evening, I walked out into the prison yard, sat down on a pile of wood and, under the glare of prison lights, slowly opened the book to the title page and frontispiece. I spent three sessions on the preface, then two whole evenings on the contents pages— three and a half pages of chapter headings with fascinating subtitles—before I even reached page one. Night after night I sat there with my treasure. Fellow prisoners argued, played cards and walked about all around me. I was oblivious. I disappeared so completely into my book that sometimes my closest friends thought I had gone bonkers.

I had started with the practical object of making my book last. But by the end of the second week, still only on page ten, I began to realize how much I was getting from super-slow reading itself. Sometimes just a particular phrase caught my attention, sometimes a sentence. I would read it slowly, analyze it, read it again—perhaps changing down into an even lower gear—and then sit for twenty minutes thinking about it before moving on. I was like a pianist studying a piece of music, phrase by phrase, rehearsing it, trying to discover and recreate exactly what the composer was trying to convey.

It is difficult to do justice to the intensity of the relationship. When Lin Yutang wrote of preparations for a tea party, I could see the charcoal fire, hear the tinkle of tiny teacups, almost taste the delicate flavor of the tea. I read myself in so thoroughly that it became not a mass of words but a living experience.

It took me something like two months to read Lin Yutang's book. By then, his philosophy on tea-making had become my philosophy on reading: You can do it fast, but it's a whole lot better done slowly. I held to the method, even after we had persuaded the Japanese to give us several hundred books from the famous Raffles library in Singapore.

The realization dawned on me that, although my body was captive, my mind was free to roam the world. From Changi, I sailed with William Albert Robinson, through his book *Deep Water and Shoal*. In my crowded cell at night, lying on a concrete floor, I felt myself dropping off to sleep in a warm cabin, the boat pitching under me. Next day, I'd be on deck again, in a storm, and after two or three graphic paragraphs I'd be gripping the helm myself, with the roar of the wind in my ears, my hair thick with salt. I wouln't let go of the helm until we sailed into the calmer waters of a new chapter. If I had read with my old momentum, it would have been like viewing Sydney Harbor from a speedboat, instead of experiencing it from the deck of my own yacht.

My voyage took me just short of eight weeks. Had I raced through the book at my former speed, I could never have experienced the blessed release of Robinson's reality becoming so vividly mine.

Sitting on a woodpile in the prison yard or crouched on my haunches in any unoccupied corner, I slow-read biographies, philosophy, encyclopedias, even the *Concise Oxford Dictionary*. One favorite was W. Somerset Maugham's *The Summing Up*. I was no longer on a rough prison woodpile, wasting away from hunger; I was in an elegant drawing room on the French Riviera, a decanter of old port at hand, listening to a great writer talking just to me about his journey through life, passing on the wisdom he had gained.

An average speed reader might dispose of *The Summing Up* in fifty minutes. But he wouldn't be living that book with the writer, as I did during the nine weeks I took to read its 379 pages. (A slow reader himself, Maugham wrote scathingly of those who "read with their eyes and not with their sensibility. It is a mechanical exercise like the Tibetans' turning of a prayer wheel.") I handled *The Summing Up* so much that it fell to pieces in the tropical heat. Then I carefully rebound it with dried banana leaves and rubber gum. I still have it, the most treasured volume in my bookcase.

I developed the habit in Changi of copying passages that especially appealed to me. One of these, from Aldous Huxley's *Ends and Means*, told how training is needed before one can fully savor anything—even alcohol and tobacco:

"First whiskies seem revolting, first pipes turn even the strongest of boyish stomachs. . . . First Shakespeare sonnets seem meaningless; first Bach fugues a bore, first differential equations sheer torture. But in due course, contact with an obscurely beautiful poem, an elaborate piece of counterpoint, or of mathematical reasoning, causes us to feel direct intuitions of beauty and significance."

I defy anyone to pick anything really significant out of a book like that by speed reading. It would be like playing a Beethoven record at the wrong speed!

Once, something I copied proved useful in camp. Our own commander had ordered us to give any spare clothing to our officers so they could appear immaculately dressed before the Japanese. The order incensed everybody. I pinned over my bunk some words from T. E. Lawrence's *Seven Pillars of Wisdom:*

"Among the Arabs there were no distinctions, traditional or natural, except the unconscious power given a famous sheik by virtue of his accomplishment, and they taught me that no man could be their leader except that he ate the ranks' food, wore their clothes, lived level with them, and yet appeared better in himself."

That night hundreds of slips of paper bearing these words were pinned up all over Changi. The affair was over, a possible nasty conflict averted.

Beyond giving me the will to survive in Changi, slow reading helps me today. Of course, super-slow reading is not for the man clearing out his briefcase or dealing with the Niagara of paper flowing across his desk. I can skim an inter-office memo as fast as the next person. But when faced with a real problem, to clear my mind of everyday clutter I will sit down quietly at home and slowly read myself into another world.

As Lin Yutang wrote: "There are two kinds of reading, reading out of business necessity, and reading as a luxury. The second kind partakes of the nature of a secret delight. It is like a walk in the woods, instead of a trip to the market. One brings home, not packages of canned tomatoes, but a brightened face and lungs filled with good clear air."

That is what super-slow reading is all about. Try it. As I read somewhere, a man is only poor when he doesn't know where his next book is coming from. And if he can get out of a book everything the author put into it, he is rich indeed.

EXERCISES

Are the people mentioned in Piddington's article familiar to you, or did you meet them here for the first time? Here are some of them: Vincent Sheean, Lin Yutang, W. Somerset Maugham, Aldous Huxley, Shakespeare, Bach, Beethoven, and T. E. Lawrence. It's not the last time you'll meet them. For they're the kind of people as familiar to the educated world (of which you're now becoming a part) as Rosie Greer and Nolan Ryan are to the sports world, and Liza Minelli and John Wayne to the entertainment world. Now consider these matters:

1. Is this a fair summing up of Piddington's point: when you don't have to read very fast, *it's better to read slowly*?

2. Is it more pleasurable and more profitable to read just that brief summing up, or to read the whole article? Why do you say so?

3. Does Piddington give reasons for his point? Results? Examples? Analogies? (Analogies are comparisons made with something else and used to make the thing compared clearer, as I used the Bible and Disneyland in my introduction to this selection.) Can you point out one instance of each of these?

4. Do they all serve to explain Piddington's point, or do they wander from it? Exactly how is his first paragraph connected with the point? (Don't say simply that it's "an introduction.")

5. Piddington has a lot to say about prison camp. Is he writing about prison camp or is he still writing about reading? Explain your answer to someone who doesn't see your point.

6. The passage Piddington tells us he copied from Aldous Huxley's *Ends and Means* is a general truth about experience. Does he offer it to us as an example of the fine passages you can spot by reading slowly? Or do you think that Piddington believes that you can apply it, not just to life in general, but also to reading?

7. Do you think Piddington did well to write his whole article on a *sentence:* "You can do [reading] fast, but it's a whole lot better done slowly"? Or do you think he could have expressed himself better and more creatively if he had written on a *topic* — "Reading"?

8. Should it surprise you that a person who thinks that "a man is only poor when he doesn't know where his next book is coming from," and who believes that if a man "can get out of a book everything the author put into it, he is rich indeed," is apparently able to keep a yacht of his own in Sydney Harbor? Explain.

If you feel that you can't provide a very satisfactory answer to some of these questions, wait. Come back to them as you near the end of the course, and try them again. Perhaps a new experience of them will be a measure of your progress.

chapter

In this and the following chapter we take up two new matters, and we will take the easier first. That is, it will be easy enough if we first concentrate on the meaning and function of some of those little words that I mentioned earlier in the book as demanding our attention— words that we see repeatedly yet may never have thought much about. We will approach the subject in a roundabout but useful way.

When two sentences or two clauses are found together, they must *belong* together—otherwise they shouldn't be together. Often two sentences or clauses that we find together belong that way because one is (a) a *cause* or (b) a *sign* of the other. Examples will make *cause* and *sign*—and their important difference—clear; first consider this one:

> Lincoln said the living could not consecrate the cemetery because it had already been consecrated by the burial there of brave men.

Here, Lincoln says that the *cause* of the living people's not being able to consecrate the cemetery is that it has already been consecrated by the brave dead. In other cases involving *cause* we are sometimes called upon to put two and two together:

> Judith cannot get the papers from her safety deposit box. The banks are closed for Memorial Day today.

/even
causes
and signs

Here we are not told—we simply have to *understand*—that the *cause* of Judith's inability to get at her safety deposit box, which is in the bank, is that the bank is closed. (There is another cause hidden in that second sentence. Can you find it?)

A *sign*, however, is different from a cause. We might say:

> That must be the military cemetery, because those identical crosses are all arranged there in lines.

Now the crosses didn't *cause* the cemetery, or cause it to be a military cemetery. What they caused was our *knowing* that what we are looking at is a military cemetery. When something is the cause, or the intended cause, of our knowing something, it is called a *sign*. The crosses row on row are a sign that military men or women are buried beneath them. Similarly we say:

> There must have been an accident at this corner. See all the broken glass?

Here, all the broken glass is a *sign* that an accident has probably taken place.

So far, you have learned no technique of reading. No, not directly. But you have focused your attention on the fact that when two sentences or clauses are found together, they belong together. This belonging together is called connection, relation, or relationship. But this relationship is not all of one kind, like that which exists between one link of a chain and another. We have therefore focused our attention further upon the *kinds* of relationship, beginning with two: *cause* and *sign*. Eventually we will consider other kinds of relationship, though perhaps it is not important that we consider them all, since our goal is essentially *alert awareness*: the awareness that between sentence and sentence there is always a relationship, and our need as readers to determine as exactly as we can what the nature of that relationship is. So if you ask yourself what technique of reading you are acquiring through the study of this and the following chapters, your answer can be: exercising a heightened awareness of relationship and the forms it takes.

In heightening this awareness, we can drill ourselves by looking at this same matter from other points of view. For instance, when you read an essay, article, or book, you surely know, and you wish to be keenly aware, that the writer is not just putting down disconnected ideas. His essay or article or book is not like a shopping list of items that have no connection: "bread, paper towels, stamps, nails, scarf." It is not like a memorandum of things to do: "Call druggist about prescription. Mail change of address to *TV Guide*. Take winter coats to cleaner." Nor is it a bunch of disconnected items about the same thing: "It's hot in summer. My birthday comes in summer. In the northern hemisphere summer lasts from late June to late September. I do not go to school in summer."

No, an article or essay or book is like a machine. A car engine is not just a box of parts: a carburetor, spark plugs, a vacuum tank, pistons, a gas tank, exhaust valves. Most of you know that all these parts must be connected, and in a particular relationship of parts, one to another. For instance, the vacuum tank draws gasoline from the gas tank for entry into the carburetor, and the carburetor mixes the gas vapor with air so that then, in each cylinder, the vapor is readily ignited by a spark from the spark plug. When that happens, the mixture explodes, thus pushing the piston. The moving pistons (through a system of rods and wheels) then move the car—which is the *point* of the whole thing.

You cannot understand the simplest gasoline engine, if you do not understand those relationships. In somewhat the same way, you cannot understand explanatory prose unless you are aware of a similar set of relationships. While we are unable at this point to give so extended an illustration of the reading problem as we gave in examining the power train of a car, we can look at two brief examples. Here is the first:

> That small growth on your face is a horny wart. The frame of your reading glasses keeps resting on that part of your cheek. You'll notice that another

growth is beginning to form on the corresponding place on your other cheek. I'll just remove it with an electric needle; there'll be no need of a biopsy.

A physician through his practiced observation has established a fact (first sentence). Then he explains the *cause* (second sentence). Then he indicates evidence—a *sign*—that the cause he has indicated is a true one (third sentence). Finally he states his conclusion—an *effect* (fourth sentence). (We'll discuss effects in the next chapter.) In this sequence of sentences the physician explains, and we understand, via the "power train" of his reasoning. Simple enough. The technique observed here we will now apply to a more difficult train of thought in our second example:

Those philosophers expressed only a theoretical doubt of the existence of a world outside their minds. They would get out of the way of a moving object as promptly as you or I. Their theoretical doubt was a doubt that that existence could be *proved.* Apparently their itch for proof was a part of their training as mathematicians. It seems not to have struck them that proof is only *indirect* evidence, that what is directly evident cannot and need not be proved, and that no amount of reasoning can make the world more evident than it plainly is.

What is the power train there? Well, what is the relationship of the second sentence to the first? If I say that the third sentence shows a cause for the first, the fourth a cause for the third, and the fifth a result of the fourth, would you agree? Wouldn't some *connectives* help us here?

There are other comparisons between a train of thought and the power train of a car—simpler ones that you can think out for yourself, like dress-making, cake-mixing, cabinet-making, or some other activity with which you are familiar. And I wish you would establish several such comparisons, for this matter of *relationship* is the crux of the reading problem, and the more devices you find to fix your attention to it the better.

So far, however, all our comparisons have been with things mechanical. You may prefer to compare relationships in what you read with living things: a simple plant, for instance, has *connected* parts— that is to say, *related* parts—for the roots (which take up water and certain nutrients), the stalk (which provides the structure, and connects roots and leaves), and the leaves (which manufacture chlorophyll for the nourishment of the plant) are not simply stuck together, but are combined in a certain order so that they communicate with one another in such a way as to sustain the phenomenon we call life.

And this—to take another step in our increasing awareness of the nature of reading matter and our act of reading it—is much like what we read. An essay, an article, or in some cases a whole book is composed of parts combined in a certain order so as to sustain the phenomenon we call *meaning*. But an engine or a plant operates without any direct attention from us—their connections, we say, are not *static* but *dynamic*: they not only exist, they work. There is a difference when it comes to a piece of reading matter. In it the relationships—which add up to the meaning—remain static, motionless, dead, until we come along and make them dynamic, make them living, by *understanding* them. And that does demand our direct attention—more or less close, according as the reading material is more or less difficult. In other words, all the connections we have been talking about must be operable, and to be operable, connections in reading material have to be understood. But understanding is an *active* process and that means *work*—more work or less, depending upon the amount of difficulty presented. Mortimer Adler, the distinguished author of *How to Read a Book*, tells us that, when we read difficult material, we can measure our growth in understanding by the amount of *fatigue* we experience from the work. "There's water under the sink! Must be a leak in a pipe." No, there's nothing fatiguing about that, though we must be aware of the relationship of *cause* if we're going to understand it. But wait till we come to the exercises, at first sight just as simple.

At this point we can stop to get our bearings. How have we advanced in our reading technique through our study of this chapter so far? We have learned that we must be attentive to *connections*—more or less attentive, according to the difficulty of the material—and that our understanding of what we read is going to depend on our understanding of those connections. In simple matters this understanding may be half-conscious and effortless; in difficult matters it must be highly conscious, and requires effort.

EXERCISE

In this exercise you need only identify all the *causes* that you can find (we will come to signs later). And in identifying the causes, don't be formal: simply point out in the paragraph anything that can be thought of as a cause of anything else in the paragraph. Finally, read the selection aloud, taking care to emphasize the contrasting elements.

> Tom's voice trembled whilst he was reading the mournful inscriptions he had written, and he most broke down. When he got done he couldn't no way make up his mind which one for Jim to scrabble onto the wall, they

was all so good; but at last he allowed he would let him scrabble them all on. Jim said it would take him a year to scrabble such a lot of truck onto the logs with a nail, and he didn't know how to make letters, besides; but Tom said he would block them out for him, and then he wouldn't have nothing to do but just follow the lines. Then pretty soon he says: "Come to think, the logs ain't a-going to do; they don't have log walls in a dungeon: we got to dig the inscriptions into a rock. We'll fetch a rock." Jim said the rock was worse than the logs; he said it would take him such a pison long time to dig them into a rock he wouldn't ever get out. But Tom said he would let me help him do it. Then he took a look to see how me and Jim was getting along with the pens. It was most pesky tedious work, hard and slow, and didn't give my hands no show to get well of the sores, and we didn't seem to make no headway hardly; so Tom says: "I know how to fix it. We got to have a rock for the coat of arms and mournful inscriptions, and we can kill two birds with that same rock. There's a gaudy big grindstone down at the mill, and we'll smouch it, and carve the things on it, and file out the pens and the saw on it, too."*

*Mark Twain, The Adventures of Huckleberry Finn (New York: Pocket Books, Inc., 1955), pp. 330–31.

chapter

The last of my questions, after a difficult paragraph given as an example in the last chapter, was whether *connectives* would help toward making it clear. Of course they would, just as they would help some other examples in the previous chapter, too. It's good to be faced with a problem, because then when a rule comes along to help you solve that problem, it appears not just as another rule to be learned, but as something you're really asking for to help you.

So far you've actually worked with four relationships: *contrast* ("wet" in one sentence contrasts with "dry" in another), *identity* ("liberty" in one sentence stands for "freedom" in another), *cause* ("I must go. It's late."), and *sign* ("Heaven's conserving on energy. There are no stars tonight."). But in dealing with helpful connectives, we'll delay our look at those that show contrast and identity, and turn to the one we've been dealing with most recently: cause.

Sometimes the writer says straight out that one thing causes another: "Air slamming together again after being split by lightning causes thunder." Or: "Use of certain vitamins and minerals causes plants to grow better." Sometimes, of course, he uses a word that means about the same thing as cause: *produces, results in, aids in, helps, creates,* etc.

But often a writer identifies the cause by putting before it a connective such as *because, since, as,* and *for:* "The ground is wet because it rained." "Since this is the evening edition of the paper, it will carry the

eight
connectives

election results." "As I was ill, I could not attend the meeting." "I want you to take your sweater, for you might catch cold again."

EXERCISES

Reread the examples just given, this time not just reading, but stopping to see that in each sentence the group of words after the *because, since, as,* and *for* is given as a cause of what is said in the remaining group of words, and that the *because, since, as,* or *for* signals that fact. Reread them orally. Here they are:

1. The ground is wet because it rained.

2. Since this is the evening edition of the paper, it will carry the election results.

3. As I was ill, I could not attend the meeting.

4. I want you to wear your sweater, for you might catch cold again.

Now that you have reread the sentences, let's consider them once again from the point of view of emphasis. You will want to emphasize *wet* (end of clause), *rained* (end of clause), and *evening* (implied contrast with "some earlier edition"). Certainly you won't emphasize *paper,* as if it were contrasted with "magazine" or "book"; true, it comes at the end of a clause, but as indicated earlier, when it comes to emphasis contrasting elements win out over endings. You will want to emphasize *election results* (end of clause), *could not attend the meeting* (end of clause), and *catch cold again* (end of clause). Probably what should be emphasized in this sentence is *cold,* and the *again* should be tucked inside the sentence so that it won't come at the end. But while a person might write "so that you won't again catch cold," most speakers wouldn't say it that way, because that way is too formal. Finally, if by *again* the writer means "still another time" or "just as you did before," then the word belongs at the end; if the writer were speaking he certainly would emphasize it: "You might catch cold AGAIN."

In doing these exercises, remind yourself of two things. First, what you are doing is not just some vocal exercise; on the contrary, you are practicing reading sentences so that they make sense—make their point. Second, you are giving to the sentences that you read exactly the same emphasis you would give them if they were your own and you were saying them in conversation. So there's nothing either routine or artificial about any of this; it's both meaningful and natural.

Here are the sentences again. Read them, emphasizing *wet, rained, evening, election results, ill, could not attend the meeting, sweater,* and *catch cold again.*

1. The ground is wet because it rained.

2. Since this is the evening edition of the paper, it will carry the election results.

3. As I was ill, I could not attend the meeting.

4. I want you to wear your sweater, for you might catch cold again.

Finally, I want you to read these sentences again just as you have read them, but with a slight emphasis also on the connectives *because, since, as,* and *for.* Just show with your voice that you are giving a little extra attention to *because, since, as,* and *for.* Go ahead.

I must give you another warning: You cannot read what follows here in the sense that you have probably understood "read" all your life, for you'll have to ask yourself at every step of the way what everything is, what everything means, exactly how things are connected, *what the point of every statement is.* But after all, isn't that our objective—by training and practice to bring you to the point where you can read and understand a page of moderately difficult English as easily and correctly as you can divide 30,834,656 by 7,136? But you can never succeed in reading if you do not proceed with it as attentively, as painstakingly, as you must if you are going to work that problem in long division. For you can never read successfully something like "*Being* is used to designate equivalency and attribution as well as both existence and the existent," if you persist in reading everything as quickly and effortlessly as you read, on the society page, an account of some couple's engagement, or on the sports page, an account of a ball game.

Earlier we said that when a writer makes two statements, one after the other, by putting them together he may mean that one is a *sign* of the other. Sometimes, of course, he says this straight out: "Wet ground in the morning is a sign that it rained during the night." Sometimes, instead, he uses some connective to indicate that relationship. One such connective is a "because" clause (or, less often, a "since," "as," or "for" clause) *with a comma in front of it:* "It must have rained last night, because this morning the ground is wet." (Contrast a "because" clause *without* a comma, which contains a cause, not a sign: "The ground is wet this morning because it rained last night." To state the full rule, *generally* when we are giving our reason for saying or thinking something, we put a comma before the *because* that follows our statement. In contrast, when we are simply stating some fact and then adding at once the cause, reason, motive, etc., responsible for that fact, we put no comma before the *because*.)

To show a sign, sometimes a writer uses some other connective like *if:* "If the sunset is red, tomorrow will be a fair day." He may also use for this purpose *when, whenever, where, wherever,* or *while:* "When the sunset is red, the next day will be fair." "Where there's smoke there's fire." "While this red light is on, the oven is heating."

Notice that the sunset does not *cause* the next day's good weather, nor the smoke the fire, nor the red light the heating of the oven. No, a sign is in some way an *effect* of that which it's a sign of: the fire is the *cause* of the smoke; the smoke is the *effect* of the fire and at the same time—and for this very reason—a sign.

I've just used the word "effect," and want now to talk a little about it. It's the *correlative*—that is, the matching term—of "cause." Perhaps this will be clearer if we look at some synonyms for each of these correlatives. A *cause* can also be known as a *reason* or sometimes a *motive;* an *effect* is also known as a *result, consequence,* or *outcome.* In any case, the cause always produces (creates, makes, brings about) the effect. The relationship we are discussing in this chapter is often known as the "cause-effect" relationship, because you can't have the one without the other. That is, something is not actually a cause unless it produces an effect, and there is no effect without a cause.

We shall come back in the next chapter to this correlation between cause and effect. Meanwhile we must pause to point out a difficulty in what we have been working with. Sometimes a clause introduced by a *when, where, while,* or *if* contains not a sign but a cause; at other times, it can simply tell us that something exists or is done at the same time or place as another thing. I am going to give you some sample sentences. In each exercise you are to tell whether the writer, by using *because, if, when, where,* or *while,* is indicating (a) a cause, (b) a sign, or (c) mere sameness in time or place.

Are the directions in that last sentence clear? I ask because I have found in the past that they are *not* clear to some students. Sometimes a writer doesn't know whether he has simply failed to make himself clear, or whether his readers are failing to pay the close attention that is the fundamental technique being taught in this course. So again: we are asking the question—is this a cause, a sign, or mere sameness?—of the clause that begins with the connective (*because, if,* etc.), and *not* of the other clause. For instance, in sentence 2 the clause "he will be of value" is clearly a *result*—a result of his learning "to read and write well." But it's not *that* clause you're being asked about. You're being asked about the one beginning with *If.* Is *that* clause a cause or a sign, or does it indicate mere sameness in time or place?

Let us glance at some more *examples.* For instance: "He must be alive because he's moving." Here, in the "because" clause—which is what we want to know about—the moving is a sign (that he's alive). Another: "When I was four years old, our President was assassinated." Here the *when* indicates mere sameness of time; your age neither caused the assassination nor was a sign of it. Finally: "If his appendix ruptures, he may get peritonitis." The *if* introduces a cause, because it's the breaking of his appendix that may cause the inflammation of the membrane lining his abdomen. So now proceed.

EXERCISES

1. He must have some infection, because his white-cell count is high.

2. If he learns to read and write well, he will be of value to his company.

3. You'll find the drinking fountain down there where all those coats are hanging.

4. The earthquake occurred while I was studying my history lesson.

5. While there's life, there's hope.

6. John Silver had to drink water because he had no rum.

7. Because my watch was stopped, I was not sure of the time.

8. While her temperature remains high, there is still some infection present.

9. While her temperature remains high, keep her in bed.

10. Where the writing is too faint, go over it again with ink.

11. Where the writing is too thick, there was too much ink on the pen point.

12. If his fingerprints are on the gun, he must have been holding it.

13. If his fingerprints are on the gun, get a warrant for his arrest.

Finally, read these exercises again. Read them aloud and slowly, while doing two things: (a) paying attention to whether you find a cause, a sign, or neither after each *because, where, when,* and *if,* and (b) slightly stressing each of these connectives as you read it.

chapter

In the last chapter we studied the cause-effect relationship and said that in this chapter we'd look at it more closely.

Effects (or results, consequences, products, outcomes—whatever word fits best) are what causes produce. When a writer makes two statements having the cause-effect relationship between them, he can (a) use a connective to indicate that one of the two is a cause (we saw examples of this in the last chapter), or (b) use a different kind of connective to indicate, instead, that the other of the two is an effect.

In his choice of connectives to indicate an effect he has a fairly wide selection: *therefore, thus, so, consequently, as a consequence, as a result, hence, whence, for that reason, because of that, wherefore, so that,* and others. To understand this use, let us look at examples of these connectives in action. Give the connective a slight emphasis as you read it aloud, and above all keep your attention on the fact that what's in the statement with the connective is the effect of what's in the other statement.

1. She had a strained ligament; therefore she could not dance in the final performance.

2. Franck was very poor, and thus, to supplement his income as organist at Ste. Clothilde, he had to go around Paris giving music lessons.

nine
cause-effect

3. The older pitcher had now walked four men, so in his stead young Walter Halas was sent to the mound.

4. I saw that Morning Star was edging up on the inside; consequently I knew that I must spur Magic Mountain on to greater effort.

5. We have recently had a heavy call for twenty-weight paper, and as a consequence do not have enough on hand to fill your order.

6. This winter it snowed heavily in the mountains; as a result, we can expect some flooding this spring.

7. We are now able to pay a larger percentage on four-year time deposits; hence, I am not renewing your two-year certificate for you until I learn whether you wish to take advantage of that plan.

8. Miranda had recently turned her attention to antiques, whence her interest in my old desk.

9. His wretched English would make a poor impression on the jury; for that reason his lawyer did not put him on the witness stand.

10. Milton did not become blind until his forties; but in this sonnet he indicates that he is not yet thirty-five. Because of that, I doubt that this sonnet is about his blindness.

11. We shall not need a new wing design for this new contract, wherefore we are giving you early notice that we do not anticipate your re-employment.

12. Mason jars became collectors' items, so that today it is hard to find one. (Note that *so that* often introduces a motive: "I'll do my homework now so that I'll have my evening free.")

In expressing the cause-effect relationship, a writer can either put a word meaning "because" before the cause, or put a word meaning "therefore" before the effect; but he doesn't do both. Thus "*Because* I could not stop for Death, he kindly stopped for me" might be reworded: "I could not stop for Death, *and so* he kindly stopped for me."

All this repetitious insistence on connectives may seem to you as tiresome as learning the multiplication tables perhaps was for you long ago, or as learning the declensions of nouns and adjectives in German or Russian may be for you today. Is it as necessary? The following story suggests an answer.

Once I was beginning to discuss in class the connective *that is.* Hardly had I begun the discussion, however, when a student raised his hand. This student was always alert, interested, cooperative, with a serious desire to learn all he could about reading and writing. Here is what he said:

"But what does *that is* mean? I always thought it was—well, just something you put into a sentence to make it sound better."

How much can be learned from his question! First, it led me to reflect how as a beginning teacher, assuming that students necessarily understood the *fundamentals* of expression, I was living in a fool's paradise. Second, I have grown to see that, despite my exhortations, even earnest students can fail to appreciate fully, or can even not notice, the very words that writers use to show how their ideas fit together to make a point. After all, to think that a writer uses *that is* so that his sentence will sound better is like thinking that an equal sign in an equation (6 + 8 = 14) is there to make the line of numbers look better! No! The equal sign is there to give the meaning intended by the person who wrote the equation. A *that is* is the same as an equal sign: "This cancer will not metastasize; that is, it will not spread," means "This cancer will not metastasize = it will not spread." (Other expressions for *that is* include *I mean, in other words, that is to say, which is the same as saying,* and *to put it another way.* If you personally have never understood their meaning, you may want to think about it now.)

Another thing we can learn from my student's question is that a writer has no way of telling to what extent his reader is following what he is writing. Though he tries to make himself understood, he can't be understood by those who don't follow his connections to get the points that his ideas add up to.

Still another thing we can learn from my student's question is— well, I hate to say it; I *feel* it's wrong, but unfortunately I *know* that it's right. It's this: some students, faced with much of what is assigned to them for reading, especially in English, don't fully realize that they are supposed to *understand* it, that it's intended to convey a meaning to them, that the writer is trying to tell them something—something that has a *point*. Instead, they read as they take some prescribed medicine, about the content and calculated effects of which they know little or nothing. In other words they read, not with any understanding, but with the idea that somehow the reading will do them some kind of good, even though they don't understand it.

As a student, you know that watching some trivial television program, or reading a comic book, or just driving around aimlessly in your car, is called wasting time. Yet none of those pastimes is a complete waste, since you get some enjoyment and perhaps some rest out of them. But what about reading an assigned essay, for instance by Matthew Arnold, without following his line of thought, without getting his individual points and seeing how they add up to the point of the whole essay? That is a *complete* waste of time. However little you may get from the agonies of Milly Snead on television or the *bam, whap, owrrk* of the comic book, you get *nothing* from Matthew Arnold if you don't understand him—not even enjoyment or rest.

I don't pretend that by studying this chapter today you will be able by tomorrow to read Matthew Arnold with understanding. But whether or not you ever read Matthew Arnold with understanding, you want to get ahead by learning to read with understanding—to get the point—of whatever expository writing you now are, or eventually will be, faced with as reading you must do.

You are even now an innately capable reader. You can read with understanding "Position the friction washer above the coupling nut, then the cone washer above the friction washer," because you know that, if you fail to follow the directions, you either won't be able to tighten the bolts or will have a leak to deal with. Yes, you're willing and able to take the trouble to find out what a coupling nut and a friction washer and a cone washer are. And you know that you can't just skim over the directions, that you have to study them carefully, and you're willing to do so. In fact, you pay strict attention to the connectives: "above," not "below," and "then," not "first." So if you want to, you can read a moderately difficult passage in expository prose, taking trouble to find out what the unfamiliar terms mean, and studying carefully instead of just skimming. Unfortunately, people have failed to grasp that a paragraph of Matthew Arnold is just as difficult, and takes just as much time and trouble, as a paragraph of instructions for repairing plumbing.

"Take out the stitches that hold the top hem in place. Along the bottom edge of the hem baste through all thicknesses to hold the welting in place." You'd take enough time and trouble with those directions to know what you're doing, wouldn't you? And if you didn't know what "welting" is, you'd find out. But you may not have learned to give the same kind of attention, time, trouble, and investigation to Matthew Arnold when he speaks of

> a perfection which consists in becoming something rather than in having something, in an inward condition of the mind and spirit, not in an outward set of circumstances.

No, you may read those words without any thought that Arnold has *said* something, has made some kind of *point*.

True, Arnold hasn't directed your attention here to something you can see in front of you—a drain pipe, a caftan. And I more than agree that the things he's talking about—"a perfection" and "a condition"— are not "things" in the sense that you can take hold of them and identify them by looking at them. (Later, I'll have a good deal more to say about this kind of difficulty.) Nor does Arnold invite you to at once go get out a wrench, or a scissors and needle and thread, or anything else your use of which will soon show you whether you have understood him or not. When, as the result of your study of them, you follow plumbing or sewing instructions carefully, you have almost immediate satisfaction by completing the plumbing repairs of the caftan *quickly*. You therefore have an immediate motive for taking care to understand the plumbing or sewing instructions, as you do not for taking the time and trouble to puzzle out Arnold's points.

As we grow older we all have to learn that some things take more time and trouble than first appeared necessary. Later in life we may make that discovery when we go to prepare our will. Earlier, we may find it out when we first have to use the long form in preparing our income tax. We don't like to think that our trouble is our own fault— some carelessness or stupidity—and it isn't. It's just a natural ignorance that is dispelled as we go through life. So I'm not suggesting that your trouble in reading somewhat difficult material is your fault. It's just that, like all of us, you must realize that certain things require more attention from you than you at first supposed. One important way to help overcome reading difficulties is learning to give this extra attention, to take this extra trouble. If you do so, you may find that a difficult writer like Arnold is well worth your while; Arnold, after all, is talking not about plumbing or a caftan, but about *you* and what you may call your life style. For these reasons, then, you may decide you can afford to be patient with the struggle we all have to go through in life. You may accept the fact that, to reach our reasonable goals, we have to turn our careful attention to things that formerly didn't seem to matter or need to be understood.

How about reading that last paragraph aloud—*as if you were explaining it to someone else?*

EXERCISE

Earlier we said that a writer, to express a cause-effect relationship, can either put a word meaning "because" before the cause, or put a word meaning "therefore" before the effect, but that he doesn't do both. For your homework, rewrite sentences 1, 2, 3, 4, 5, 6, 7, 9, 11, and 12 (skipping 8 and 10) on pp. 66–68 with a word for "because" in front of the cause, instead of the word for "therefore" that now indicates the effect. Vary the words you use. Notice that you'll have to change the semicolons to commas. When you have rewritten the sentences, read them aloud, observing which words should get emphasis.

chapter

A bright man who sneers at his own and other people's schoolteachers may seem to you much like a big boy who torments little boys—in other words, a bully. But suppose the bright man isn't so contemptuous of schoolteachers as he seems; suppose he's being at least partly playful for a comic effect, calling teachers pedagogues somewhat as a young man playfully calls his young wife an old woman. Suppose, moreover, that even if he is still partly serious, his real purpose isn't just to make fun, but to encourage some schools to improve themselves. Such a man is called a satirist (put the accent on *sat-*), and what he writes is called satire. All this is relevant here not so as to increase your capabilities as a reader (though it will do that), but to prepare you to understand a short passage by H. L. Mencken, a passage in which big words, sometimes incongruously coupled with colloquial words, contribute not only emphasis but comedy—comedy that is meant to produce satire.

Likewise to understand the passage, you should recall not only that sparkling Burgundy is a bubbling wine, but also that Mencken impudently implied its praiseworthiness at a time when wine was prohibited in the United States by law. You will also find helpful the following pieces of information: President Harding had received an honorary title of Doctor of Laws from some college or university, but no one called him Dr. Harding except Mencken, who hoped the learned title would emphasize that Harding was an *unlearned* man. Living on the Eastern seaboard, Mencken would have considered Marion, Ohio—

ten
getting
the point

Harding's hometown—to be virtually the backwoods (or so Mencken pretended), and rural Tennessee, which he mentions later in the passage, to be the same even more so. Mencken thought of the Elks as an organization simple enough for Harding to understand thoroughly. *Con amore* is a direction to musicians meaning "with love." (The orchestra on television's Fright Night used to play *con amore*—for the same comic purpose that Mencken has in using the term *con amore* here.) Since *late* means "recently dead," Mencken's intention in applying it to the poet Dante, who died in 1321, is apparently comic. Diplomats, of course, train themselves not to betray hostile or contemptuous feelings. The Institutes of Justinian are an old but historically important collection of court decisions and principles of law; the writer implies that a backwoods judge, unlike a learned one, would know nothing about them. A "schoolma'am" is a female pedagogue. Finally, Addison is an English writer who was once considered a model for other writers.

Now study the following passage carefully. You may need a dictionary to get Mencken's meaning here of *infallibly, nub* (see under *nib), style, stylist, assiduously, range, meditation, ideals, obscure, formulate, disjected, tibia, enigmatical, cacophonous, invest* (of the several meanings, be sure you have the one that makes sense here), *literate, bombard, filched, unaffected* (again, be sure you have the meaning that fits), *essay* (as a verb that fits), *Balkan, state* (one meaning of *state* as an adjective), and perhaps other words. By *self-conscious,* Mencken probably meant "conscious" in one of your dictionary's meanings of the word *conscious.*

"What a lot of work," you say, "for a page or two of reading!" Certainly. Wouldn't you expect to do an equal or greater amount of work on a page of mathematics? Is reading easier than mathematics? Well, here is the passage; let's see.

BURGUNDY OR MUSH?

H. L. Mencken

One of the most widely enjoyed essayists of the 1920s, H. L. Mencken is the author both of standard authoritative works on the American language and three amusing volumes of reminiscences, Happy Days, Heathen Days, *and* Newspaper Days. *Long associated with the* Baltimore Sun *papers, with George Jean Nathan he also edited the* American Mercury.

1 What is in the head infallibly oozes out of the nub of the pen. 2 If it is sparkling Burgundy the writing is full of life and charm. 3 If it is mush the writing is mush too. 4 The late Dr. Harding, twenty-ninth President of the Federal Union, was a highly self-conscious stylist. 5 He practiced prose composition assiduously, and was regarded by the pedagogues of Marion, Ohio, and vicinity as a very talented fellow. 6 But when he sent a message to Congress it was so muddled in style that even the late Henry Cabot Lodge, a professional literary man, could not understand it. 7 Why? 8 Simply because Dr. Harding's thoughts, on the high and grave subjects he discussed, were so muddled that he couldn't understand them himself. 9 But on matters within his range of customary meditation he was clear and even charming, as all of us are. 10 I once heard him deliver a brief address upon the ideals of the Elks. 11 It was a topic close to his heart, and he had thought about it at length and *con amore.* 12 The result was an excellent speech—clear, logical, forceful, and with a touch of wild, romantic beauty. 13 His sentences hung together. 14 He employed simple words and put them together with skill. 15 But when, at a public meeting in Washington, he essayed to deliver an oration on the subject of the late Dante Alighieri, he quickly became so obscure and absurd that even the Diplomatic Corps began to snicker. 16 The cause was plain: he knew no more about Dante than a Tennessee county judge knows about the Institutes of Justinian. 17 Trying to formulate ideas upon the topic, he could get together only a few disjected fragments and ghosts of ideas—here an ear, there a section of tibia; beyond a puff of soul substance or other gas. 18 The resultant speech was thus enigmatical, cacophonous, and awful stuff. 19 It sounded precisely like a lecture by a college professor on

style. 20 A pedagogue, confronted by Dr. Harding in class, would have set him to the business of what is called improving his vocabulary—that is, to the business of making his writing even worse than it was.

21 Dr. Harding, in point of fact, had all the vocabulary that he needed, and a great deal more. 22 Any idea that he could formulate clearly he could convey clearly. 23 Any idea that genuinely moved him he could invest with charm—which is to say, with what the pedagogues call style. 24 I believe that this capacity is possessed by all literate persons above the age of fourteen. 25 It is not acquired by studying textbooks; it is acquired by learning how to think. 26 Children even younger often show it. 27 I have a niece, now eleven years old, who already has an excellent style. 28 When she writes to me about things that interest her—in other words, about the things she is capable of thinking about—she puts her thoughts into clear, dignified, and admirable English. 29 Her vocabulary, so far, is unspoiled by schoolma'ams. 30 She doesn't try to knock me out by bombarding me with hard words, and phrases filched from Addison. 31 She is unaffected and hence her writing is charming. 32 But if she essayed to send me a communication on the subject, say, of Balkan politics or government ownership, her style would descend instantly to the level of that of Dr. Harding's state papers.

Now first I want you to reread the Mencken passage, so as to prepare to answer these questions: Mencken is not really writing about—making a point about—schoolteachers, Harding, Dante, the Institutes of Justinian, or his niece; what then *is* he writing about? That is, what's his topic? Can you already tell me in one word of your own? And what is *Mencken's* word for that topic? (It's one of the words that I suggested you might have to look up.) I'll ask you some more about this later; meanwhile, reread the passage and ponder the questions just asked.

EXERCISE

Now let's return to connections and connectives, and do this exercise.

1. In sentence 1, which half is the cause, and which the effect?

2. In sentence 2, which half is the cause, and which the effect? What connective does Mencken use to indicate the cause? Answer the same questions for sentence 3. With what word in sentence 2 is the first "mush" in sentence 3 contrasted? With which one is the second "mush" contrasted?

3. If Mencken had used a connective in sentence 4 to connect the rest of the paragraph with what has gone before, which of the

following connectives would he have used: *therefore, the reason is that, for example, however?*

4. Sentence 6 begins with the connective *but*. *But* means, in general, "From what I've just said, you'd expect such and such. Instead, you find something else." Usually, it means that instead of the expected cause—or result—you find a different cause or result, or perhaps *no* result. In this way *but* (and its synonyms) is a kind of opposite of both *because* and *therefore*. Sentence 6 says Harding's messages were muddled in style. What then in sentence 5 would make you expect the opposite of that—which answers the question, why did Mencken use here the connective *but?*

5. What cause does Mencken then give for the fact that Harding's messages were muddled in style? With what connective does Mencken show that he is giving it as a cause? (Obvious though the answer seems to me, many students find this question hard.) And what does the question "Why?" (sentence 7) tell us is going to follow?

6. In sentence 9 Mencken again uses *but*. You will see why he does so if you can answer this question: What do "matters within his range" and "clear" contrast with in sentence 8? Do sentences 6, 8, and 9, taken together, come down to the same thing as sentence 1? Give particular attention to the last question because, as I think you'll see later, it's at the very heart of the reading problem. (Pretend, at least, that your instructor is requiring you to do this work in class. That will encourage you to do all the tedious—but extremely valuable—turning back to the passage that this lesson requires.)

That last question is in fact so important that I want to make sure you have the answer right: By "What is in the head" Mencken means, of course, a writer's ideas and the way they're put together—his thinking. What comes "out of the nub of the pen" are his words—his writing. Since what was in the writer Harding's head was muddled (sentence 8), what came of the nub of his pen was necessarily muddled, too (sentence 6). But in sentence 9 what's in Harding's head is the kind of thing he's used to thinking about clearly, so that what issues from the nub of his pen is also clear.

Do you also see now that sentences 2 and 3 are only extensions of the idea of sentence 1, and furthermore that they are reflected in sentences 6, 8, and 9? When what was in Harding's head was mush (unclear ideas), what came from his pen was mush, too. But when (sentence 9) what was in his head was the sparkling Burgundy of his clear thinking, what came from his pen was likewise sparkling charm. (Mencken actually uses the same word—*charm, charming*—in sentences 2 and 9.)

Now explain to yourself, or to your instructor if he wishes, how sentences 10–14 reflect sentence 2 (and therefore sentence 1). Explain how sentences 15 and 16 reflect sentence 3 (and therefore sentence 1). Explain how sentences 17–19 do the same thing. Go even down into Mencken's second paragraph and show that sentence 22 says exactly what sentence 1 says. The only difference is that sentence 1 is a *general* truth—that is, true of anybody; but if it is true of anybody then it is true of the *specific* (particular, individual) person Harding. In sentence 22, therefore, Mencken is able to apply sentence 1 to Harding. And Harding at the same time is an *example* and a *proof* of sentence 1—as shown throughout Mencken's first paragraph.

Finally, show how sentences 29–32 say the same thing as sentences 2 and 3 (and therefore sentence 1), and note how Mencken, having used Harding as his first example and proof, now uses his niece for another example and proof.

You should now see a vast difference between the way most students write and the way experienced writers such as Mencken write. No, the *real* difference is not that Mencken and other writers you read have a bigger vocabulary; it is not that they know from American history and other fields more people and things that they can talk about; it is not that the flow—the style—of their language is smoother.

Instead, the real difference is this: too often, most students go about writing as follows. First they think of one idea about their topic and put it down. Then they think of another idea about it and put that down. Then a third, and so on. But in contrast, the writers you read— when they aren't telling you how to make or do something, or telling you a story—do just the opposite. They put down an idea about their topic and then, instead of next putting down another idea, they put down the *same* idea again. Then they put down that same idea again and again and again, until they reach the end of their article.

Now an untrained reader does not recognize that the writers he reads are putting down just one idea again and again. The untrained reader thinks he's reading *different* ideas, one after another. *You* didn't realize, did you, the first couple of times that you read Mencken's two paragraphs, that he was repeating the same idea again and again and again? You had the impression, did you not, that he had maybe twenty or thirty ideas, and that he wrote them down one after another? One reason untrained readers think of an experienced writer's one repeated idea as a list of different ideas is that, in repeating his one idea, he gives it first one wording and then another, and applies it first to one case or example and then to another. Look and see how Mencken has done exactly that in his paragraphs.

If you are studying this book and not just reading it, you must follow directions faithfully, and see how all I say about the selections we are reading is so. You have to keep explaining to yourself the things I point out, and keep proving things to yourself. If you haven't been doing that in my whole discussion of Mencken's two paragraphs, turn back and begin to do so now. You will find the whole problem of reading—and the solution—right in these two paragraphs and the analysis that follows them. So back to work!

Notice that Mencken first says that what's in the head oozes out of the pen. That's his general, his broadest statement. Then he becomes a little more specific: he gives us two kinds of things that can be in the head, and the two matching things that can ooze from the pen. He says that either thought like sparkling Burgundy is in the head—in which case the writing that oozes from the pen will be clear and lively—or else that thought like mush is in the head, in which case mush will ooze from the pen. Then all that follows keeps repeating that what's in the head comes out of the pen: either Burgundy (Harding's knowledge of the Elks issuing as his clear address on the subject, and the niece's capable thoughts issuing as clear English), or else mush (Harding's ignorance of matters of state issuing as muddled writing; his ignorance of Dante issuing as an "awful" speech on Dante; and any child's ignorance of Balkan politics or state ownership issuing as no better than Harding's worst writing).

Now comes the most important question of all. A while back I remarked that Mencken isn't really writing about schoolteachers, Harding, Dante, the Institutes of Justinian, or his niece. And I asked you to ponder what he *is* writing about, what his topic is. What did you decide, or what have you since decided? Perhaps you answer that Mencken's topic here is *writing*, and that's a good general answer. Mencken's word for his topic, as you notice, is *style*. (If you yourself haven't arrived at that answer, go back and quickly reread Mencken's paragraphs, to verify that his topic actually is writing, or style.)

But now for the important point—the most important single fact that you can learn about reading (and writing). *No one can really write explanatory material about a topic. One must write a sentence about the topic and then write the whole article or theme or paper about that sentence. In other words, one must first make some point about the topic and then write the paper entirely on that point.*

The most important question you have to answer about Mencken's article—or about any piece of explanatory prose you read—is this: What is the original sentence that the writer wrote about his topic? Here, which statement is Mencken talking about all the way through his article? Or to put it another way, what's the *point* of the whole article? Tell the point first in Mencken's own words, as found in the article; then, if you want, put it in your own words.

We've already seen clearly, have we not, which statement Mencken is talking about all the way through his article. That must be the key sentence that he originally wrote about his topic, that must be his *point*. And what is it? His *first* sentence, not surprisingly: "What is in the head infallibly oozes out of the nub of the pen." Of course Mencken restates his point less poetically—and less comically—in the second paragraph, as we've already noticed: "Any idea that he could formulate clearly he could convey clearly." True, he says that about Harding, but since Mencken picked Harding only as one specific example to illustrate the general rule, we can see that he means this: "Any idea that anybody can formulate clearly in his head he can convey clearly in his writing."

How would you put the idea in a sentence of your own? (It's always a good test of whether you understand something to try to put it into your own words.) How about this: "Good clear writing is and can be only a reflection of good clear thinking."

Do you see now what I mean when I say that if you can't state the point of something you've read, you haven't really *read* it, haven't really understood it? But if you can say, "Yes, I get the point," in a real sense you have understood what you read, even though some details remain vague. (Details like why Mencken picked Henry Cabot Lodge as his example of a professional literary man; what Mencken means when he says Harding had a great deal more vocabulary than he needed; and what Balkan politics are like.) So make it a rule to always find the main statement that any writer makes about his topic, and keeps writing about all the way through. Some people call that main statement the central idea; others call it the theme sentence; still others, the thesis statement. You may find *point* a good name for it.

No, we are not through with Mencken's two paragraphs. Bear in mind that we're really *reading* them, not just passing our eyes over them. And Mencken's paragraphs, if we really read them, reveal a few more things of interest.

First, as you discovered, Mencken is writing about writing, so what he says should be of interest to us as students of reading, since writing and reading are two sides of the same coin. We notice this fact in the paragraphs themselves, where the reader of the writing described as good or bad is always in the background, and actually comes into the foreground both in the person of Henry Cabot Lodge, who couldn't read Harding's messages to Congress with understanding, and in the person of Mencken himself, who isn't bombarded "with hard words, and phrases filched from Addison," when he reads letters from his niece. (By the way, we shouldn't overlook how this mocking satirist's loving pride in his little niece, and the warm relationship that leads to her writing letters to him, modifies his *tone*.) If reading and writing are two sides of the same coin, Mencken's point, as we've seen, is that the coin itself—the gold or silver that gives it value and binds the front and back together—is *thinking*. And we ought to reflect that the thinking that the writer has put into his writing can be extracted only if the reader, too, is thinking as he reads. (And that is exactly our point as we go through this book, is it not?)

But does Mencken add anything more specific about writing to his general statement that what's in the head comes out of the pen? Yes, he does. On the positive side, he describes good writing as writing in which *the sentences hang together*. Of course it wouldn't do any good for sentences to hang together, if the reader didn't see that they hang together, and how. That is why we, in analyzing Mencken's own paragraphs have been careful to see how his sentences hang together on a single strand: the idea that what's in the head comes out of the pen. For what comes out of the pen has to get back into the (reader's) head, if real *reading* is being done.

On the corresponding negative side, Mencken describes bad writing exactly as I described many students' bad writing: first one idea on a topic, then another, then another, and so on. Thus a student writing on the topic "the telephone" might say that the telephone was invented by Alexander Graham Bell; that it's a great convenience; that it's faster than mail; that sometimes it wakes you up when you're asleep; that often you find that the caller has a wrong number; that push-button telephones are faster than dial telephones; that long-distance calling can become expensive. This student writes badly because he didn't first make one statement—write one sentence—about the telephone, as for instance, "The telephone is convenient," or "The telephone is a nuisance," and then keep writing about that statement to the very end. The student's mistake is precisely what Mencken describes Harding as doing when Harding wrote about Dante. Harding took "Dante" as a topic and put down first one idea about Dante, then another, and then another—"disjected fragments," as Mencken put it, "here an ear, there a section of tibia"—instead of making at the beginning *one* statement about Dante, and then writing only about that statement to the very end.

One can read Harding's oration on Dante, or the student's theme on the telephone, only as you can "read" a grocery list or a page of the telephone book. For by real "reading" I mean reading for the point, and obviously a grocery list, or a telephone book, or a list of miscellaneous facts about the telephone or Dante—"disjected fragments . . . here an ear, there a section of tibia"—can make no point. My point here, of course, is that if you read any article as if it were just a list of ideas, you're no better off than if you were trying to "read" the student's theme about the telephone or Harding's oration on Dante, or a grocery list, or a page of the telephone book. In other words, you're not really reading. Real reading is seeing how a writer's sentences hang together to make sense, to make a point.

I've been emphasizing how Mencken's sentences hang together to make a point because they all express the one idea that what is in the head comes out of the pen. But here's something that at first seems contradictory: Mencken's point is not some secret that no one ever discovered before him. Other writers had said the same thing before him; in fact, that writing is thinking on paper is obvious—it's just common sense. What's different about Mencken's statement of it, what freshens it and lends interest to it, are the examples he chooses to illustrate it: Harding's muddled state papers; college professors (who, when they are more interested in their image as college professors than in the patient help they ought to be giving their students, are always amusing figures); the Diplomatic Corps; a Tennessee county judge; and so on.

In fact, if you had read a lot of Mencken, you would strongly suspect that—even though he was writing on his point about style (if he weren't, he wouldn't have an article but just a list)—he was at least as deeply interested in his examples as in the point itself. Indeed, those who know much of Mencken's work can see how he used these paragraphs as a shooting gallery in which he set up some of his favorite targets—the presidents of the 1920s, the South, the Middle West (Main Street, if you will), colleges and universities—to take pot shots at.

That, then, is the apparent contradiction: Mencken wrote, as he should have, on one point, yet perhaps his real interest lay not in that point but in his incidental, miscellaneous material. As a student of reading you don't have to solve the problem presented by that apparent contradiction; yet even without solving it you can learn something from it:

First, writing an article on just one sentence doesn't make the article mere repetition. On the contrary, the examples, the details, the illustrations, the reasoning make it varied and rich. And so, even though reading for the point is your object, this variety gives more point to your reading, for it would be a pity to neglect this richness, which most often is precisely what makes an article *interesting*.

Second, you must nevertheless notice that Mencken does not stop what he's doing—making the point that good writing comes from good thinking—to talk about Harding, the Institutes of Justinian, his niece, and so on (just as I am awfully tempted now to stop and tell you how important was the rediscovery of the Institutes of Justinian in the Middle Ages). No, he doesn't drive off on any side roads to pick wildflowers. On the contrary, he uses whatever he says about Harding, his niece, and so on to express perfectly his point that good thinking makes good writing. And you must read his paragraphs as he wrote them: you must take what he says about Harding, his niece, and so on not primarily as important in themselves, but as mere illustrations of Mencken's point (that only what a person can think about clearly and well can he write about clearly and well). True, some of Mencken's material—like his assertion that Harding, in his awful oration on Dante, sounded like a college professor lecturing on style—doesn't dovetail quite so smoothly into the adjoining material. But that's because I've lifted Mencken's paragraphs from a much longer article, and you would have to read the whole article to understand exactly how everything fits.

EXERCISE

As a final assignment on this long chapter, read Mencken's two paragraphs aloud, emphasizing the things he contrasts, emphasizing the ends of his sentences. and giving some slight emphasis to his connectives. Then read his paragraphs silently to yourself as if you were *hearing* them. If you've followed all the instructions in this chapter, I think you'll find that you're understanding the two paragraphs very well.

chapter

Whenever you reach the stage of reading ability where you can understand Mortimer Adler's *How to Read a Book,* I hope you'll read it. You'll find some continuity between my book and his, and in his you'll learn more about reading than there's time to teach you here. I'm going to give you five paragraphs of Adler's book because they make good material for a drill on some of the principles of reading you've learned so far. But at the same time they constitute a key passage in Adler's book and hence, naturally, a key concept in understanding the art of reading. You'll derive double profit, therefore, if you take an interest in the exercise that follows the paragraphs.

Before you read Adler's paragraphs, however, I want to prepare you in several ways. First, when Adler speaks of the symbols on the page, he means the printed words on the page. Second—and this regards his meaning—he indicates that when you understand something at once, you don't *increase* your understanding because, he feels, you already have an *equivalent* understanding in your head; otherwise you wouldn't grasp effortlessly what's being proposed to you. I myself would put it this way: lifting weights that you can lift effortlessly isn't going to increase your muscle power. Third, among the wrong things that Adler says you can do when you don't understand a book at once, is turning to two forms of outside help. You may argue that this book of mine is exactly that kind of outside help! But I presume Adler would agree that at your stage of reading you do need outside help in learning the fundamental techniques you must know, before you can ever

eleven
making
progress

approach the kind of reading he has in mind. Fourth, you can gather from Adler's paragraphs a truth that was stated expressly elsewhere in his book: the more *work* reading matter takes, the more you get out of it—the more it improves you. I'm sure he doesn't have in mind reading matter that's hard because it's badly written; but he would have to include the kind of reading where the writer leaves it up to the reader to supply illustrations and examples. What Adler has directly in mind, however, is matter hard to read because the concepts are difficult and because the line of reasoning requires tiringly close attention.

Here then are Adler's paragraphs. Read them carefully and thoughtfully.

from HOW TO READ A BOOK
Mortimer Adler

Long associated with the Great Books program, Mortimer Adler has recently edited with Charles Van Doren the Great Treasury of Western Thought, *which Jacques Barzun has called a "storehouse of clear and exact utterance."*

1 Here is a book, . . . and here is your mind. 2 The book consists of language written by someone for the sake of communicating something to you. 3 Your success in reading is determined by the extent to which you get all that the writer intended to communicate.

4   Now, as you go through the pages, either you understand perfectly everything the author has to say or you do not.   5   If you do, you may have gained information, but you could not have increased your understanding.   6   If, upon effortless inspection, a book is completely intelligible to you, then the author and you are as two minds in the same mold.   7   The symbols on the page merely express the common understanding you had before you met.

8   Let us take the second alternative.   9   You do not understand the book *perfectly at once*.   10   Let us even assume—what unhappily is not always true—that you understand enough to know that you do not understand it all.   11   You know there is more in the book than you understand and, hence, that the book contains something which can increase your understanding.

12   What do you do then?   13   You can do a number of things.   14   You can take the book to someone else who, you think, can read better than you, and have him explain the parts that troubled you.   15   Or you can get him to recommend a textbook or commentary which will make it all plain by telling you what the author meant.   16   Or you may decide, as many students do, that what's over your head isn't worth bothering about, that you understand enough, and the rest doesn't matter.   17   If you do any of these things, you are not doing the job of reading which the book requires.

18   That is done in one way only.   19   Without external help, you take the book into your study and work on it. 20   With nothing but the power of your mind, you operate on the symbols before you in such a way that you gradually lift yourself from a state of understanding less to one of understanding more.   21   Such elevation, accomplished by the mind working on a book, is reading, the kind of reading which a book which challenges your understanding deserves.

You will grasp the significance of the questions in the following exercise, and perhaps recognize in them a method to improve reading (even writing) skills, if I explain to you the purpose behind these questions, which otherwise might seem trivial and tedious. Remember how at the beginning of the chapter I indicated that one of its purposes is *drill* on principles of reading you've already learned. (How often must the golf pro tell the learner, "Keep your head *down!*") This is in fact one of the techniques of reading that we've learned and are drilling on here: becoming increasingly aware of how a writer of explanatory prose states an idea, then restates it again and again and again till the end of his composition, varying only the particular ways in which he presents it. Which is drill (so to speak) disguised. All the same, there is progress in his thought, and the principal ways he makes you aware of the direction of that progress are (a) the use of the little words (like *since, therefore,* and *whereas*) that indicate what particular connection he is making between statement and statement; and (b) emphasis.

Emphasis is a subject that might fill a whole book. Simply using a word as the subject, verb, or object of a sentence emphasizes that word. Putting an idea in a main clause instead of a relative or subordinate clause emphasizes that idea. Placing any item out of its normal place in a sentence directs attention to it, hence emphasizes it. Interrupting the normal flow of a sentence often serves to emphasize what comes directly before (and sometimes after) the interrupter. Even varying, or not varying, the construction and the length of succeeding sentences subtly conveys emphasis, and therefore meaning. A dash can convey emphasis. So, naturally, can underlining (italics). But since we could go into all these only in a book entirely devoted to emphasis, I assume that if, through drill, you get a rather lively sense of emphasis itself, you will begin to grasp naturally, as you go along in your own reading, those many devices of emphasis that we are unable to treat.

So here we are drilling yet again on those devices of emphasis that we have already treated. I won't delay you further by explaining my choice of these. Suffice it to say that they are emphasis by contrast (with identity or similarity serving as a background), and emphasis by position (last or first).

Still, the techniques of using all these things are not an end in themselves; they are only devices to help a reader in his progress toward getting meaning, toward getting the *point*. These questions, therefore, also drill you by requiring you to show the connection of ideas whereby the writer is explaining his point. True, you would slowly increase your grasp of the importance of *getting the meaning* as you continued to read by yourself—especially by being required to derive meaning from your assigned study in some other courses. The purpose of all this drill, then, is to enable you to take a giant step ahead. Work seriously, therefore, on the following questions. They will contribute substantially to your progress—progress that you yourself, I think, can sense.

EXERCISES

1. What word will you certainly emphasize in sentence 4? What *two* devices of emphasis (in line with the meaning, of course!) serve to indicate that you should certainly emphasize that word? What eight words will you emphasize because they are in contrast with that word?

2. Sentence 5 begins "If you do." If you do *what*? In sentence 5 what two words are equivalent to each other and what two words are contrasted with each other? Read the sentence aloud now, with proper emphasis.

3. What in sentence 4 is equivalent to "completely intelligible to you" in sentence 6? What in sentence 7 is equivalent to "minds in the same mold" in sentence 6?

4. What part of sentence 4 is sentence 9 equivalent to? The first part of sentence 11 corresponds to the end of what previous sentence? And to the whole of which previous sentence? To what part of sentence 4 do these all correspond?

5. When is "then" in sentence 12? "Parts that troubled you" in sentence 14 is equivalent to what in sentence 10? In sentence 9? In sentence 4?

6. "Make it all plain" in sentence 15 is equivalent to what in sentence 14? "What's over your head" in sentence 16 is equivalent to what in sentence 11? In sentence 10? In sentence 9? In sentence 4?

7. What *is* "That" in sentence 18? Is sentence 18 equivalent to the second half of sentence 19? What expressions in sentence 19 are equivalent to what expressions in sentence 20? In sentence 20, what expressions remain the same and what expressions change (are contrasted)? Read the sentence with the proper emphasis.

8. What elements in sentence 21 are equivalent to what elements in sentence 20? What in sentence 20 corresponds to what in sentence 17, and is this an equivalency or a contrast?

9. Would you or would not you say that the point of the passage is that reading matter which at first you don't entirely understand will increase your understanding, if you yourself work on it till you figure out what the writer is trying to tell you? Does Adler—like Mencken in the previous chapter—tend to repeat his point over and over (from positive and negative points of view)? Study Adler's paragraph and see.

10. Reread Adler's paragraphs thoughtfully, carefully, and aloud.

chapter

What you have been studying is *reading*, and not clear style as the result of clear thinking, or anything else that you have been reading *about*. But now I want to discuss miscellaneous matters. Some of them have been staring us in the face, but so far I've said nothing directly about them. Others need review. To add to the miscellany, I'm going to give you some of what instructors often call "motivation."

The first matter is a reading problem. Since a writer of explanatory prose has to write on one point only, it shouldn't be surprising to find the same thing, in different guises, appearing over and over again in what we read, and to observe that this repetition makes up the writer's paragraphs. But when we come to actual selections, do we really find this kind of writing?

I think you can answer that question, and we can make a principle of your answer: a writer can introduce as many ideas, and write about as many things, as are necessary or useful in explaining and defending the one point on which he's writing, so long as he makes clear the connection between all his material and that one point. For instance, let's say a writer is writing on the point, "Nature is *not* fickle." He could say that opponents of his point rest their case on Heisenberg's uncertainty principle, which he might then have to explain. That might well lead him into reference to subatomic particles, their behavior, and measurements of that behavior. Then he might insist that it is not the

twelve
sticking to
the point

behavior of those particles that is erratic, but their measurement—
erratic because the measurer, so to speak, gets in his own way, can't
help his own activity's affecting the measurement. To bolster his case,
he might sketch Einstein's theory of how to get around that difficulty.
Here are many ideas! But as long as he can show they are attached
constructively to his point—and *how* they are attached—he has not
gone astray.

Just in case you're not convinced that a writer must write—and
does write—on one point, imagine this situation: you're reading some
instructions on how to clear a stopped-up drain in your kitchen, and
just when the writer of the instructions has told you to hook up a
garden hose in your back yard and bring the nozzle end in through the
kitchen window, suddenly he begins telling you about his garden hose
and the different nozzle adjustments he uses for different flowers, and
then about the flowers themselves—how his roses are doing, and what
plant food he's feeding his lilacs.

In such a reading experience you would be momentarily confused,
then indignant: Why doesn't the writer stick to the point?

Do you suppose, then, that a writer who is writing about something more difficult, more abstract, more literary, or more theoretical, is
magically excused from having a point and sticking to it? Do you think
that just because he's writing about pollution, nutrition, love, or

growth differential in immigrants and their children, it's somehow logical and right for him to include material not clearly related to his point? Of course you don't!

What has all this got to do with you as a reader? As a reader, naturally you have to find out what the writer's point is, but then you must also see how everything the writer says in his essay fits in with that point. You even have to answer the question, what particular point is he making at this or that particular stage in his article? And exactly how does that particular point fit into the general point of the whole?

I don't mean that these questions constitute some kind of mystery or puzzle; the writer has done his best to give you the answers. No, I've used the expressions *have to find out* and *answer* and *questions* because reading has to be a very active process: the writer is guiding your thinking, but you have to *do* the thinking, have to keep turning your mind in the directions where the writer is pointing. For a writer might just as well not have any central point in his article, if you fail to understand it as central; and he might just as well not have the parts of his article connected to the central point, if you fail to pay attention to the connections.

True, in this book I'm giving you a reading course, not a collection of more or less interesting articles that you supposedly know how to read already—or can magically learn to read just by reading. I'm attempting to take the place of the more difficult authors and to explain what they're doing step by step, so that your reading techniques will be formed exactly on their writing techniques, somewhat as you learn to type by learning first how the inventors of the typewriter arranged the keyboard.

It is also true that you could apply to your own writing the essential things that all these authors are doing: stating the point of their article; stating the particular points of their various paragraphs and sections, and showing how those points help to explain the point of the whole article; furnishing those points with abundant examples, illustrations, and reasons; and never, never just writing at random about "a lot of things," but carefully showing the connection of the parts with the whole. So it is true then, too, that this book should be of very great help to you when you turn to your writing lessons, since it shows you how practiced writers apply the same most necessary rules of writing that you have to apply when you write. But despite all that, this book is arranged primarily as a reading textbook.

It is true also that a good writing course is naturally of help to you when you turn to your reading lessons. By writing clearly and logically yourself, you will see all the more plainly how the writers you read guide your mind in the same ways that you use to guide your readers' minds.

So much for the connection between reading courses and writing courses. They are closely allied, cover largely the same principles, and are two sides of the same coin—the coin of thinking. They are valuable adjuncts to each other. But in this book we are learning *reading*. How much have you learned so far?

It would be good to review at this point some of the principles—aside from those already reviewed in this chapter—that I hope you've not only learned, but even begun to make a part of yourself. The first principle is that what you read has a *point*. An explanatory article is written because the writer wants to tell you something, wants you to get that point. What he writes is like a column of figures that add up to something, and not like a jumble of numbers written every which way on a page. Then it's up to you to do your best to get that point—to follow his addition of one plus two plus three plus four to see that they do equal ten.

But the process of getting a writer's point demands close attention; it demands more or less hard work, just as mathematics problems do. Yet you must realize that there's a *point* in your doing the hard work. Just as you're willing to take the trouble and time to follow a writer or speaker who's telling you how to make a macramé belt or handbag, or how to adjust the idle screw on your car or change a flat tire, so you must be willing to take the trouble and time to see why a writer says that war is biologically undesirable, or that the real purpose of government is to protect our rights.

For if it's worthwhile to take care with things that we wear, and to take care of your car, how much more worthwhile it is to take care of your mind. For when, through careful and thoughtful reading, you grow in the habit of *understanding*, you improve not your clothes or car or house or lawn or boat or hi fi, but *you*.

While acquiring and perfecting their car, clothes, lawn, or boat—things outside themselves—people may neglect the self-development that comes from careful, thoughtful reading, may neglect the perfection of their inmost, truest selves, their *minds*, and thus overlook what Matthew Arnold speaks of as

> a perfection which consists in becoming something rather than in having something, in an inward condition of the mind and spirit, not in an outward set of circumstances.

Believe me, you'll find this more important than the better grades you'll earn through learning to read, and the greater earning power you'll have later on because of increased capacity to understand written communication.

Another closely related thing I hope you've learned is that careful, thoughtful reading takes patience and *time*. You may, in fact, have to take the time to reread and reread and reread (it's wonderful how the simple process of rereading can produce or increase understanding). The encouraging thing is that if you're willing to take the time at the beginning, reading—good reading—will go faster and faster.

Among the things that take the most time—to come to another principle that I hope you've learned—is looking up in the dictionary the words you don't know, and then, out of the several meanings given by your dictionary, figuring out which meaning makes sense in the sentence you're reading. You'll have even more difficulty with the capitalized nouns you keep meeting in your reading; for instance, when a political writer in a news magazine tells you, "He is doing just what Bismarck was too shrewd to do," it doesn't help you much to learn from the dictionary that Bismarck was the first chancellor of Germany. In fact, the sentence itself tells you more—namely, that Bismarck was shrewd—if you're alert enough to pick up the information.

I'm sure you've grasped the fact that the writer isn't writing here *about* Bismarck; he's using what he says about Bismarck to explain something else—namely, his point. For another necessary principle of reading that we've considered is this one: though a writer may talk about a lot of things in explaining his point, we're not to confuse those things with the point itself.

Among other things that you must keep in mind is the constant interplay, in what you read, between the elements that stay the same and the elements that change or are contrasted, as for example:

> *Jack Spratt* could eat no *fat;*
> His *wife* could eat no *lean.*

This interplay, as you've seen, is a basic factor in communication; it's the very warp and woof—the very texture—of language. Things that change must be emphasized, mentally and vocally, if you're going to get a writer's point, and I hope you're forming the habit of emphasizing them.

Other things that you should emphasize habitually are the *endings* (where the point usually lies) of clauses and sentences. But as we saw, *beginnings* too often deserve some emphasis, and so do *connectives.* You must keep on paying close attention to the little words and phrases that writers use as connectives, for every time they use them writers make some kind of point; to grasp that point, you must decide what *relationship* a writer is indicating by his choice of connective between two words or groups of words. Since the whole universe, down to its tiniest parts, is made up of *causes* (which are often reasons or motives) and *effects* (which are often signs), the cause-effect relationship is one that you must always be on the watch for.

I'll close this chapter with two principles of a different kind, which so far have been mostly implicit in this book. The first is that unless you personally have chosen something to read strictly for entertainment, your main concern should by no means be whether you *like* or *dislike* a writer's article. For the writer is not saying to you, "Look at what a good article I've written," or "I'll interest you if it kills me." He's saying, "Here's my point. Let me explain it." So the question is not whether you like the article but whether you understand it. Anyone can like or dislike; only the one who has done the real work of reading can understand.

The second principle implicit in this book somewhat resembles the first. It's this: at least for the present, don't read to see whether you approve or disapprove of what a writer says. You may indeed happen to agree or disagree, but don't read *for the purpose* of agreeing or disagreeing. Read for the purpose of understanding, of following a writer's line of argument, of grasping his point, of examining his evidence.

Why do I say this? First, because it's as easy to have an opinion as it is to write out a check for a million dollars—and the ease ought to make you suspicious. Second, many people seem to feel an obligation, even a compulsion, to have an opinion on anything and everything. Should criminals convicted of atrocious crimes such as murder be paroled? If I ask that question in class, everybody in the room *knows* whether they should or shouldn't be (except me: I must confess that I don't know at all). The trouble is that some *know* they should be paroled and some *know* they shouldn't—a fact that again ought to make you suspicious.

Third, you have no real grasp of your own opinion if you haven't seen the opposite opinion presented in its strongest and clearest form; and if you cannot bear to look patiently and fairly at the opposing evidence, *that* should make you suspicious. Fourth, it's a sobering thought that if a prospective juror admits to having formed an opinion on the case coming up, the court doesn't permit him to be among those who will decide *on the evidence* of the accused's guilt or innocence. Fifth, let me ask you whether you've ever *changed* your opinion. Finally, sixth, since this is not a course in opinions but a course in reading, here at least the question will always be "What's the writer's point?" and not "What's your opinion?" It's all too easy to switch from the harder question—what does the writer say?—to the much easier question—what do *you* say?

Good reading is rereading. For your assignment, make this chapter an exercise in reading. Reread it *aloud,* then at the end of each paragraph close your eyes or look away, and *explain to yourself* the point of each paragraph. You won't be looking for the point of the whole chapter, of course, because it's actually a review of many chapters.

chapter

In this chapter you'll study a full-length article, originally written as an address to American high school principals. The vocabulary is not difficult; nevertheless, I want to make sure that you know the meaning of the following words, so I am listing them with definitions that tell you what each word means as used in the article. Please study them; then as you read the article, refer to them at need. Such a presentation of vocabulary is not always advisable; we have not used it elsewhere. However, it is standard in many textbooks; see whether it works well for you here.

acquisition   getting

agitation   excited demand for change

aptitude   special talent

artisan   workman; craftsman

aspiration   desire; hope

assimilate   learn

attainment   what a person has accomplished

bred   created

cite   refer to; point to

colleague   member of the same profession as one's own

comprehensive   covering the whole thing

thirteen
close
reading

conception   idea of things or of something

contemporary   someone or something about the same age

crucial   at a point where things must go one way or the other

decentralized   allowing local choices rather than running things
from one center

derogatory   implying a low opinion of

elementary   beginning; earliest; simplest; basic

embrace   include

emigrant   one who leaves a country to live elsewhere

engaged in   busy with

essential   necessary

harmonious   working together

immigrant   one who enters a country to live there

infamous   widely thought of as bad, or hard

lamentable   regrettable (accent on lam-)

optimum   best possible

platitude   too familiar to need stating

relevant   having to do with us or with what we are talking about

review   take a close, new look at

sheer   nothing but; absolute; plain and simple

speculation   guesswork

succession   replacement; series

tradition   way of looking at or doing things that is shared with others, present and past

unique   only one of its kind

utterly   completely; to the limit

vigilance   keeping an eye on someone

Perhaps you wonder where the exercises are for so long a chapter? What is the "feedback" to be? The questions follow immediately each unit of the article, along with commentary. Don't be disturbed because this is an unusual place for questions in a textbook; there is a reason for putting them there. As you study the article—especially if your instructor breaks it up into several assignments—you may be glad you're not called on to answer all those questions *at the end.*

ENGLISH AND AMERICAN EDUCATION
Sir Geoffrey Crowther

Sir Geoffrey Crowther—later Lord Crowther—was editor of the London Economist *and held many important educational posts in England. He died in 1972.*

1   For the past three years I have been engaged, with my colleagues of the Central Advisory Council on Education in England, in a comprehensive study of the English educational system. I had some of my own education in the United States, and I have been a frequent visitor to America ever since. This double experience has bred in me a growing sense of astonishment that two countries which share the same language, so many of the same cultural traditions and ways of life, whose political, religious, and social aspirations are so largely identical, should have educational systems so utterly different as to provide almost no basis for a comparison between them.

[Why the introduction? The reason for the first two sentences is that Crowther wants to show us at once that he's in a good position to know what he's talking about. (He introduces himself impressively, yet in fact modestly: he doesn't even hint that for a dozen years he was the editor of the distinguished London Economist.) But note how he uses his double experience both to show us his credentials and to move directly to his point: *English and American education are different.* Is his title a sentence or a topic? As he presents his point in the first paragraph, is that point a sentence or a topic? Explain at length. Note that the point is a very simple comparison, yet one on which he'll build his whole article. His *whole* article—that fact is of immediate importance for us, for we have finally reached the point of analyzing an article *as a whole*. Recalling your study of the Mencken and Adler excerpts, what can you predict about the simple comparison just referred to?]

2 That is a strong statement, and my present purpose is to try to justify it. Let me first say, however, that I have no intention whatever of trying to show that one national system is, on balance, better than the other; only that they are much more different than is usually realized.

[In this short paragraph Crowther does five things of interest to you as a student of reading. First, he tells you that he's going to write on a statement—a sentence—about his topic, not just about the topic. Second, since he declares that his purpose is to justify it to you, he's emphasizing that it is indeed his thesis statement or central idea. Again, what *is* that central statement? Is his purpose to tell us that he's on an educational council? To tell us that he's often visited America? To tell us that the English and we speak the same language? He does *say* those things, but is that what he's *telling* us? Some students have difficulty with these questions, yet distinguishing between the point and what is not the point is essential. Let's stop a moment for an analogy:

You go into a store, get some chewing gum, pay the cashier, and go on your way. Was your purpose to pay a visit to the store? You *did* visit it. Was your purpose to give the cashier some money? You *did* do so. But what was your purpose? Out of the several things you did, what one thing was the point of all you did? (Your instructor may at this point suggest a brief discussion of the difference between *means* and *ends*.)

Third, Crowther supplies a reason for assembling all the facts that make up his long article: to say that the educational systems in two very similar countries are utterly different is "a strong statement," perhaps a surprising one, too, and whoever makes it should back it up in detail.

Fourth, he directs your precise attention to the wording of his thesis statement: he says nothing more nor less than that the two are *different*; he does not say that one is *better*. That's the very thing a listener or reader satisfied with vague, sweeping impressions and not used to examining precise wording might miss; so he promotes clarity from the start by making sure you won't look for what is *not* in his article and, thus distracted, fail to see what *is* there. In other words, he wants to make sure you'll be *reading for the point.*

You want to make sure, too. You may wish to argue mentally with Crowther. You may want to deny that the two systems are different, or argue that the American system is better. Does Crowther deny that it's better—for the United States? You may wish to argue that the English system is unfair to English children. Do the great majority of the English people—who are the ones affected—feel that way? Or do you wish to argue that the English people "just don't know any better"?

How well does the English system work? (Not "How well do you think it would work?"—which is "opinion," rearing its ugly head again.) Do you know enough about how it does work to argue about it? In fact, how well does the American system work? Do you really know enough about *that* to argue about it? So what's there to argue about? Crowther has told us that the English nation through his committee have taken a long, critical look at English education and modified what they found wrong with it. Has the United States ever done that? Does that leave us in a good position to argue?

Finally, even if there is something to argue about in Crowther's article, do you really want to take on an educational expert, a former editor of one of the world's most distinguished publications? Personally, I'd rather leave that to, say, the president of Harvard or the chancellor of Berkeley, or the current American expert on American and European education, Dr. James D. Koerner. If you *learn* what Crowther—and, of course, many others—have to say, later as a voter and taxpayer you'll be in a better position to take a long, critical look at the American system and decide what in it may or may not need modifying. Besides, later on you'll have a good deal of *experience* of how the American system is working and won't have to fall back on "opinions." (Often criticized by my superiors in the past for "failing" to tell my classes what *I* think, let me dodge such criticism by saying that I would call the American system of education what President Herbert Hoover called Prohibition: a noble experiment.) But it all comes down to whether you're reading Crowther for his *point:* the two systems are different. His point is not that one or the other system is better. You misread him if you think he's challenging you to a debate.

Fifth, at long last—and here I think is the English touch—with the same sentence Crowther executes a master stroke of diplomacy: knowing that his listeners and readers feel at a disadvantage when confronted with so urbane and accomplished a speaker, and that they may feel hostile because they expect him to argue (and perhaps prove) that something American is not the very best, Crowther reassures them at once that his purpose is to do no such thing. So they can all relax and listen to what he's saying, instead of being distracted by rejecting automatically everything he says. Even some of those who are twice as American as anybody else suddenly find that Crowther is a nice man, with his heart in the right place, and they sit back and prepare to enjoy him.]

3 The American and the English educational systems are different in purpose, structure, and method. Let us start with purpose. The two systems grew up in response to very different pressures and needs. In America, you have always been very conscious of the need to build up a new society. You have wanted to construct something bigger, richer, better than you have. This is said to arise from something in the American national character, but that seems to me to turn the logic upside down; it is the American national character that has arisen from the circumstances in which the American people have found themselves. From the start it was necessary to create a supply of ministers of religion, of lawyers, and of skilled artisans—I place them in the order of importance in which they were regarded at the time. Later on there came the obvious necessity of incorporating the great waves of immigrants into your society. Still later came the great task, in which you are still engaged, of knitting your varied economic, social, and racial groups into the harmonious and balanced society in which the principles of democratic government can work properly.

[Crowther begins this paragraph with an extremely important sentence. It's important for two separate reasons. First, after he's said the two educational systems are different, he could think of dozens of differences. Can he talk about them all? What would you get if he did list a long catalog of differences? Would you get *information* from such a catalog? Would you get from it an *understanding* of what makes the two systems different, discussed in a way that makes the difference worth talking about? You may decide that common sense dictates that he limit his discussion to a few ways in which the two systems are different, and that he pick differences *that make a difference*—differences out of which he can make a *point*.

Now since *purpose* must always govern everything (I don't mean that having a good purpose ever makes it all right to use bad ways to achieve that purpose), Crowther does well to start with purpose. But purpose immediately dictates *structure,* and they both immediately dictate *method* of use. That's easy to see: a tin shears and sewing scissors obviously exist only for their purposes. Because they have different purposes, will they be differently constructed (structure)? Because of their different construction and purpose, will you have to operate them differently (method)? So in picking purpose, structure, and method, has Crowther made a logical choice?

The second reason for the importance of that sentence—especially to us as students of reading—is that it sets up at once a structure for

Crowther's article that we'll find very easy to follow. When he adds at once "Let us start with purpose," do we know at once which of the three sections he'll be discussing there? Do we gather that in the following section he'll discuss difference in structure? And in the final section—what?

Glance ahead now at the first sentence of paragraph 12 and of paragraph 18. And notice how those sentences act as signposts to tell you that a new section is beginning. When you've done that, let me add that under each of these main divisions he'll have subdivisions (which we'll deal with later), and each will have a signpost just as the three main divisions do. That's because Crowther, besides telling you about English and American education, keeps remembering to tell you where you are in his article, *so that you can follow his line of thought easily.* As a student of reading you must grasp the importance of noticing such signposts and using them in following the line of thought in articles you read.

Finally, notice similar signposts within Crowther's paragraph: *from the start, later on, still later.*]

4 Consciously or unconsciously, American education has at all times been designed to serve these social purposes. It has been regarded as an instrument by which society can build its own future. From its nature, it has inescapably been concerned with the rank and file of the people. Its chief concern for many generations has been to do something to the masses—and I think the word is *to,* not *for*—in the interests of the American dream.

[Crowther begins his next paragraph with the summarizing expression *all this,* meaning all that he's just said. A summary of any kind is usually a signal that a writer is about to turn to another, though of course related, matter. As you see, he's been talking about the purpose of education in the United States; now he's turning to the purpose of education in England. Does that form a contrast? As you also see, he makes a deft transition by associating both the old and the new material with the idea of *well known (platitude, familiar);* that is, the idea of *well known* is the link to which both the American and the English purpose are linked, though the one is linked positively and the other negatively ("What may not be quite so familiar"). Thus Crowther has created a neat, clear transition.]

5 All this, of course, is platitude in America. What may not be quite so familiar is the contrast in the historical situation in England. We have never been very conscious of the necessity to build a new society. At all relevant times we have had a fully developed society already in being. And at all relevant times we have also, I am sorry to say, been on the whole pretty

satisfied with the society we have. For most of the last two hundred years, American education has been designed to do a job of construction; English education has been designed primarily for maintenance, with improvement coming second. In the very latest period, perhaps, those attitudes have started to change. As with so many aspects of education, there seem to be the first signs of a tendency to change sides. Your education is becoming socially more conservative just when ours is becoming more consciously radical.

6 But that is a speculation for the future, on which I will not enlarge. I am talking of the influences of the past, which have shaped the structures of today. American education has always had to concern itself with the common man in his multitudes. The concern of English education has until very recently been with the maintenance of society, in the words of the old prayer which you will often hear in school and college chapels, "that there may never be wanting a succession of persons duly qualified to serve God in church and state." This is a conception which does not necessarily embrace the education of the great mass. There is a fine, rich, broad educational tradition in England. But it is not a tradition of education, above the minimum level, for the multitude. Post-primary education has always been thought of as a privilege in England; it was not until 1944 that the principle of secondary education for all was established, and it is hardly yet fully effective.

[In the following short paragraph 7, which I want you to glance ahead at and read, Crowther is not talking about his topic at all. Then what is he talking about? Why does he write this paragraph? What kind of paragraph is this?

I hope you already have the answers, which go something like this: Crowther writes this paragraph just for the purposes of keeping his line of thought clear in your mind. So of course it's a variety of the typically short transition paragraph, in which, for the reader's sake, he's talking about the construction of his article rather than about the subject matter of his article. And he's saying, in effect, "Now I'll still be talking about what I've just been talking about. But I'm going to introduce a twofold subdivision, which I'll both prepare you for and help you identify by calling one subdivision the shocker and the other a favorable surprise." Then in the first sentence of paragraph 8 he keeps on making sure that you're with him by saying, "I will start with the shocker." Read on now and see.]

7 Let me pursue this contrast a little further. Let me give you two of the consequences, of which I would guess that one will shock you, while the other may perhaps surprise you more favorably.

8 I will start with the shocker. The consequence of our different attitude is that the sheer size, the volume or quantity, of English education is very much smaller than American. The age at which the legal compulsion to attend school expires is still only fifteen. Moreover, that is an effective leaving age, and more than four children out of five in fact leave school before they

are sixteen. Of the sixteen-year-old age group—those between their sixteenth and seventeenth birthdays—only 22 per cent are still in full-time education. In the seventeen-year olds, the figure falls to 13 per cent of the boys and 11 per cent of the girls. Among eighteen-year-olds, it is 8 per cent of the boys and 5.5 per cent of the girls.

9 What strikes Americans, I find, as even odder than these figures is the fact that we are not, as a nation, greatly disturbed by them, although many of us think they ought to be larger. But we cannot assume that public opinion is on our side. I am very doubtful whether there would be any support in public opinion for a policy of keeping the majority of children in school after sixteen, and I am certain that you would find hardly anyone in England who believes, as you do, in keeping all children at school until eighteen. Our college students represent about 3 per cent of each age group, and there is an expansion program in hand that will raise it to about 5 per cent. Anybody who suggested that we needed any more than that would meet with the strongest resistance, and not least from the universities themselves.

10 This attitude does not arise from any lack of love for our children. It is not because we think we can't afford it. The proportion of our national income that we spend on general welfare services—social security, health, and the like—is about the highest in the world. It is not from lack of generosity or lack of means that we confine education after the middle teens to a minority. It is because we sincerely believe that it is the right thing to do, in the interests of the children themselves. After all, there can be no absolute rules about education. Nobody believes that any child should be allowed to leave school at twelve. I do not suppose a time will ever come when, even in America, it will become legal or compulsory for everyone to stay in full-time education until twenty-five. Where you fix the age between those limits is surely a matter of judgment. And why should it be the same age for all children? Our belief in England is that, balancing what can be got out of school against what can be got out of life, the average boy or girl has probably had the optimum dose after eleven years of schooling—and do not forget that we begin, by legal compulsion, at the age of five. Eleven years, after all, is one year out of every six or seven of the average lifetime.

[Perhaps Crowther can be said to give you next a little intelligence test. He begins "Now let me give you the other side of the medal," and we note that he's talking here about his subject, to be sure, but also marking a stage in the development of his writing—and, of course, of your reading. So his sentence is transitional, or connective. That's clear enough. But what was the *first* side of the medal? In other words, what particular stage in Crowther's article does this sentence mark?]

11 Now let me give you the other side of the medal. Because education after fifteen or sixteen is confined to a minority, that minority gets every assistance that the state can provide. It is nowadays, to an overwhelming extent, a minority chosen for intelligence and attainment. There are, of course, still the independent schools, where very substantial fees have to be

paid. But the pressure of numbers upon them is such that a stupid boy or girl will have great difficulty getting in. And in the state schools, selection is by merit only. But once selected, a boy finds himself with his foot not so much on a ladder as an escalator. He will have the best resources of the best schools concentrated on him. If he can secure a place in a university, and that also is a matter of selection by merit, the state will pay his tuition fees and his living expenses, not only during the session but during his vacation as well. There is no such thing as working your way through college in England. We do not need a National Merit Scholarship scheme because we have one already. Nor is this a recent thing. It has been expanded in recent years, but it has always existed.

[In the next paragraph Crowther moves on, as you've already observed, to the second of the three main divisions of his article. But there, and in what follows, I want you to notice another matter to which I've already alluded: subdivisions. There are three of these here. The first is introduced with the words *the outstanding difference;* the second with the simple word *second;* and the third with words also reminding us that we're still in the section on structure—*the other great difference under the heading of structure.*

Crowther calls centralization the outstanding difference perhaps because it's at the root of the other two, national financing and the principle of selection. But what does he put in the most emphatic place? First, what *is* the most emphatic place? When you glance ahead to see, notice also how many paragraphs he expends on this difference. How many paragraphs did he expend on each of the other differences? Would you suppose that greater length ordinarily signals and produces greater emphasis? Does great emphasis on one difference suggest that *this* difference is the one that makes the most difference?

But what I want to direct your attention to is that Crowther *signals* the beginning of each subdivision, and that he does so for your benefit, so you'll keep his line of thinking clear. The less attention you pay to his signals, of course, the less help they'll be to you. Read on now. When you've digested the next six paragraphs, I'll have you glance back to discover something new.]

12 Let me move on to structure. The outstanding difference here lies in the fact that we have a very much smaller degree of local control than you do. There are about 50,000 school boards in the United States, each of them, I suppose, more or less free to run the schools as it thinks best. That gives a total population in the average school board area of about 3500 persons. In England there are about 130 local education authorities, which gives an average population per area of about 300,000. Moreover, there are two other differences, apart from this sharp difference in size. Your school boards consist, I believe, in most states, of persons specially elected for the purpose, with no other duties. In England the schools are run by the county council, or the borough council, which is the general purpose government of the area.

13 Second, your school boards raise their own money by direct taxes, or at least the greater part of it. In England about 70 per cent of the expenditure of the local education authorities is met out of grants from the central government in London. There are advantages and disadvantages in this. It means that we do not have the enormous range in standards between rich areas and poor areas that you do. It means a much greater degree of standardization of conditions of employment among the teachers, and therefore of interchangeability between school and school and between area and area. But it also inevitably means a greater degree of uniformity imposed from the center. We think our system is decentralized, because it allows much more local freedom and variety than exist in the school systems of most Continental European countries. But there is no doubt that it is much more highly centralized than the American system.

14 The other great difference under the heading of structure is the principle of selection upon which our system is based. All children, except the minority in fee-paying schools, go to undifferentiated schools from the age of five to the age of eleven. At eleven or thereabouts, a proportion of them, varying from area to area but averaging between 20 and 25 per cent, is selected for what we call grammar schools, which include children to the age of eighteen, though not all the pupils stay that long. The remainder go to what are called secondary modern schools, which include children to age fifteen and increasingly to sixteen, but no older.

15 You will see from this description that the crucial time for an English child is at the age of eleven or a little more. The selection test then applied— the famous or infamous eleven-plus examination—is supposed to be a classification purely by ability and aptitude, without any suspicion of being derogatory to those who are not selected. But, of course, everybody wants to be selected, and with the growing pressure of numbers as a result of the post-war bulge of population, the selection has been getting steadily more competitive. As the result of agitation, the Labor Party has adopted the policy of abolishing the eleven-plus examination by sending all children at that age to the same schools, the so-called comprehensive secondary schools. The Labor Party has moved toward this system in several of the areas where it controls the local council, and even in Conservative areas there is a distinct movement to experiment with systems that do not involve sending children to different schools at the age of eleven.

16 I have several times seen this movement quoted in America as evidence that English education is turning away from selection. I think this is a grave misunderstanding. The public objection to selection at eleven is social and political, not educational. It is an objection on the part of parents to having their children sent to different schools, not to their having different educations. And the remedies that are being applied are wholly in terms of institutions, not in terms of the education they provide. I know, for example, one large new comprehensive school built by a Labor council. Every child entering that school is tested and placed in one of fifteen "streams," differentiated by the children's intelligence and aptitude. This selection is done by the

teachers; the parents have nothing to do with it; and the children are not even supposed to know which stream is which in intelligence grading. A child placed in one of the top streams will have an almost wholly different education from a child placed even in one of the middle streams. If this is not selection, I do not know the meaning of the term. But this is what we mean by a comprehensive school. Many people in England will tell you that the comprehensive school has been copied from the American comprehensive high school, some meaning it as a compliment, some as the reverse. I have often told them that they could hardly be more mistaken.

[Is what Crowther is driving at in that paragraph clear to you? It was not clear to me until I studied the paragraph searchingly several times, attempting to *visualize* the schools described.]

17 Nonselection—if that is the opposite of selection—as it is practiced in America is totally unknown in England. By nonselection I mean the principle of treating all children alike, allowing them to sort themselves out by their choice of courses, by what they find easy and difficult, or by their varying ambitions—with counseling assistance, no doubt, but without any compulsory segregations. I am sure that your system seems as odd to us as ours does to you. There is no retreat from selection in England; the only change is that a growing number of people—but still a minority—think that the selection should be within a common school, not between schools.

[Now glance back at the expression *these figures* in the first sentence of paragraph 9. What figures does Crowther mean? Yes, the percentages he's been talking about in the preceding paragraph. Now look at *This attitude* in the first sentence of paragraph 10. What attitude? Described where?

Again, in the first sentence of paragraph 11 you will find *the other side of the medal*. What does this refer to earlier in the article? Is this a reference of identity, repetition, or contrast? What does the use of the word *other* signal? Paragraph 12 begins, *Let me move on to structure.* What signpost does that match in a previous paragraph?

Paragraph 13 begins with *Second* and *school boards.* If what follows is second, what must it be matched with in the preceding paragraph? *What* school boards is Crowther talking about in this second of two paragraphs? Where do you look for the answer? In paragraph 14, *The other great difference* takes you back to *second* (paragraph 13) and *The outstanding difference* (paragraph 12), which mark the previous subdivisions in this section. And what does *this description,* which appears in the first sentence of paragraph 15, match? Where do we find what it matches? Now go to the beginning of paragraph 16 and find *this movement.* What movement? And to what does *nonselection* at the beginning of paragraph 17 refer, and where is it discussed?

Can we make a rule based on all that evidence? Yes, there is a rule—almost as invariable as the rule that a sentence must begin with a capital letter: *in the first sentence of each new paragraph of expository prose, the reader must be able to put the point of a pencil on at least one word or expression that refers to something in the preceding paragraph—or sometimes, if the new paragraph begins a new section or subdivision, on an expression that refers to the preceding section or subdivision.*

The expression just mentioned may well be a connective like *therefore* or *nevertheless* or *for* (the *for* meaning "because"). But it can also be an item that in some way matches or connects with anything in the preceding paragraph. Such items include *synonyms* (identities), *pronouns* referring to nouns in the preceding paragraph ("Betty Ford . . . she . . . "), *antonyms* (opposites), and *phrasal transitions* ("Now we can logically turn to . . .").

Knowing about those focusing tactics should produce an excellent reading (and writing!) technique. Always be conscious of what in a new paragraph matches or in any way connects with something in the preceding paragraph. Thus your reading technique will follow along perfectly with the rule that the writer is following.

All trained writers scrupulously observe this rule precisely because you the reader must see easily and quickly how the line of thought carries on from paragraph to paragraph—in other words, see *the connection of ideas.* You the reader must grasp the connection between the idea of the new paragraph and the idea of the paragraph you've just read. Of course the more alert you are to the way a writer is observing this rule, the more easily you will understand him.

And now you'll see that Crowther begins his last section. Since he speaks of four points, we can expect four subdivisions. Glance ahead to see whether you can find where each begins. If you can't find them all, I'll help you: the first begins in paragraph 19, the second in paragraph 22, the third apparently in paragraph 24, and the fourth in paragraph 26. Do read the first sentence of each of these paragraphs before you read through the whole of the passage that follows.]

18 The differences between the two countries in educational method make an enormous subject, and I must restrict myself to four points out of many that it would be possible to make.

19 The first of these differences in method lies in the position of the teacher, in the relative positions of the teacher and the textbook. One of the things about American education that most strikes the English visitor is the importance you attach to textbooks. We have no parallel to that. To begin with, I do not think there are more than two or three, at most, of the local education authorities in England that tell their schools what textbooks to use.

That is left to the teacher, occasionally the principal, or the head of department in a large school. And in the higher grades, more often than not, there is not a textbook at all. A teacher will often recommend a book as covering the subject pretty well and as being useful for reference but will not make any attempt to go through it chapter by chapter.

20 This system places a much greater responsibility on the individual teacher, and I have often been asked in America whether we do not have a lot of trouble with it. So far as the political and social responsibility of the teacher is concerned, I cannot recall having heard of a single case arising through a teacher's being accused of using a book which seems offensive or objectionable to somebody in authority. That is partly, perhaps mainly, because our system of large authorities and rather remote and indirect public control puts the individual teacher largely out of the reach of vigilance committees, whether of parents or of the local chamber of commerce. There is also a strong tradition against anything that smacks of political interference with the schools.

21 Educational responsibility, however, is another matter. Quite clearly, a system like ours, which places so much responsibility on the individual teacher, cannot work well unless the average standard of intelligence, knowledge, and teaching competence is high. Up to the present, we have been able to maintain that standard. It is partly, of course, a matter of numbers. In the whole of England last year there were only some 260,000 schoolteachers. We were a little short, but 300,000 would have given us all we need. And this is in a country about one quarter the size of the United States. I do not know how many schoolteachers there are in the United States, but I am very sure it is many more than four times 300,000. I do not see how you could possibly have coped with the enormous increase in the American school population in the past forty years without being willing to take thousands of young men and women who needed close support from a textbook before they could teach. Indeed, under the pressure of rising numbers in the schools, I fear we shall find before long that we shall have to give the teacher more assistance, and that implies more external control on his teaching. This particular contrast is now, however, entirely a matter of numbers. It is partly also the result of a different tradition of teacher training, which, in England, has always laid a much greater emphasis on the content of what is to be taught than in America and much less on questions of pedagogic method.

22 The second difference in method is the absence in England of the course system which is so universal in your schools and colleges. Indeed, the word "course" has a wholly different meaning in the two countries. If you asked an English school child what courses he was taking, he wouldn't know what you meant. If you asked him what subjects he was taking, he would answer English, Latin, mathematics, history, and so forth. But that would not mean, as it would in America, that those were the subjects he had chosen to take. They would be the subjects that his form, or class, was taking, and therefore that he was taking with the rest of the class. Until the boy is about fifteen or sixteen, it is unlikely that he or his parents have had any say in the choice of form in which he is placed. And at no age does he have any say in deciding the curriculum of that form. At the higher ages, there is a choice between three or four different curriculums, but each curriculum has to be taken, within narrow limits, as it stands.

23 Here, indeed, is a contrast with the American system. Perhaps it is not quite so sharp a contrast in practice as it is in principle, as I observe that, more and more, those American boys and girls who have ambition to gain admittance to a good college find their choice of courses in high school made for them by the college entrance requirements. But there is one important consequence for teaching that is worth bringing out. In an English school, in any year but one (and that one is what we call the fifth form year, about the age of fourteen or fifteen), you can assume that the pupils who are taking a subject in one year will be taking the same subject next year. The study of a subject can therefore be planned as a continuous process over a period of years. That is what we mean when we use the word "course." We mean a whole balanced curriculum of six or seven or eight subjects, planned to continue over three or four or five years. Once a boy or girl enters on such a course, he or she will normally pursue it to the end. And all the boys and girls in a course will take substantially the same subjects, with perhaps slight options, as between a second classical or a second modern language. You will therefore understand how bewildered we are when we contemplate one of your neat, packaged, self-contained, nine-month courses, such as high school physics. It is no good asking an English schoolboy when he enters college how many years of French he has had at school. Two boys might both truthfully answer nine years. But they might mean totally different things, and neither one would mean what you thought he meant.

24 How, then, do we measure what a student has accomplished, if we cannot count up the number of courses he has satisfactorily taken? The answer is that we rely, to an extent wholly unknown to you, on general examinations. Every year—sometimes every term—the pupil has to take a written examination in all the subjects of the curriculum, and his further progress depends, sometimes entirely, on his performance in that examination. Most of these examinations are set and assessed within the school itself, by his own teachers. But at three crucial points in his career the examination is set and assessed by an external body. The first of these is the eleven-plus examination, which determines to which sort of secondary school the child should go. The second comes at fifteen or sixteen and is called the Ordinary Level of the General Certificate of Education, set and assessed by one of nine examining boards closely associated with the universities. This examination can be taken in any number of subjects from one upwards, but the most usual practice is to take it in from five to nine subjects. Third, there is the Advanced Level of the General Certificate of Education, which is taken at eighteen or thereabouts and which plays a large part in university entrance.

25 I have been describing the practice of the grammar schools; that is, the schools for the brightest 20 to 25 per cent of the children. Examinations, especially written examinations, play a much smaller part in the life of the less intelligent children. Even in this case, however, they play a much larger part than they do in America; and there is a rising demand for public examinations, at lower standards of intelligence than those of the General Certificate of Education, for these less gifted children. I cannot honestly say that the children themselves clamor for examinations, but employers do, and therefore so do the parents. All the questions that Americans ask and answer in terms of the number and variety of courses a student has taken we ask and answer in terms of the examinations he has passed.

26   I have left to the last what is the sharpest difference of all between our two systems. This is our system of specialization, in which England is, I think, unique in the world. A student will take the examination for the Ordinary Level of the General Certificate of Education at the age of fifteen or sixteen in a wide range of subjects drawn both from the humanities and from the natural sciences. But once he has passed that examination, he will specialize. That is to say, he will devote two thirds, or perhaps even more, of his time in school to a narrow range of subjects. In one boy's case, it may be physics, chemistry, and mathematics; in another's it may be chemistry and biology, or it may be history or modern languages and literature, or classical languages and philosophy. But, whatever the choice, the greater part of the pupil's attention, in the classroom and in his private study time, is given to his specialty, and he will take the advanced level examination at eighteen in his special subjects only. When he gets to the university, the specialization is even more intense. The range of subjects does not usually get any narrower, but the student gives 100 per cent of his time to it.

27   I have found that to Americans, and indeed to educationalists from every country in the world except England, this seems a very strange system indeed. Perhaps you will have difficulty in believing that I really mean what I say. So let me cite my own case, though it is now more than thirty years old. I was a modern languages specialist. For my last three years at school, from the ages of fifteen to eighteen, I studied mostly French and German language and literature, perhaps three or four hours a week of history, and one hour of Scripture on Sundays. For another two years at Cambridge, even the history and the Scripture were cut out, and I studied French and German exclusively. Five years of my life were given to those languages. My experience was perhaps a little extreme; I think the admixture of general and contrasting subjects would nowadays, in a good school, be a little bigger. But the difference would not be great. The English boy or girl is a specialist from the age of fifteen or sixteen.

28   The advisory council of which I am chairman was specifically requested by the Minister of Education to review this system of specialization. We examined it most carefully and discussed it at great length, both with witnesses and among ourselves. In the end we came to the conclusion that we wanted to see it continued. We found that it was being pushed too far, and we have made a number of suggestions for removing what we think are abuses. But we have reported in favor of this system of specialization. And that is a unanimous conclusion reached by a council made up of educators of all kinds. Perhaps you will find that fact as extraordinary as the system itself, and I must try to give you some of our reasons for thinking that, in this matter, we in England are in step and the whole of the rest of the world is out of step.

[Notice that in paragraph 29 Crowther introduces another two-part subdivision. With what words does he signal that a two-part division follows? The first part he takes up at once; the second he treats in paragraphs 30 and 31. Since these three paragraphs that follow are the best part of Crowther's article, the part that you yourself, even though you're in an American school, can profitably adapt to your own career as a student and to your attitude toward your studies, I'd like you to read them carefully and ponder them deeply.]

29 Let me begin by telling you of one argument that we reject. That is the argument that every intelligent citizen, or every educated man, ought to know something about each subject in a range so wide that it compels a balanced curriculum; that no one can afford to be ignorant of history, government, science, languages, and so forth. To this, we would give our answer in two parts. First, it is true that there are certain elementary skills and knowledges that everyone must have—reading, writing, arithmetic, and several more. But these essential elements can be, and should be, provided by the age of sixteen. If you go on with them after that age, you will be wasting your time, because the knowledge you instill will be forgotten unless it can be attached to the main intellectual interest of a boy's or girl's life, which begins to emerge at about that age.

30 The second part of the answer is that it is only when you have got these essential elementary skills and knowledges out of the way that you can confront the real task of education. The acquisition of factual knowledge is by itself a poor test of any education and a lamentably poor test of the education of boys and girls of seventeen and eighteen. It has been said that the process of education is not to be compared to that of filling up an empty pot, but rather to that of lighting a fire. The proper test of an education is whether it teaches the pupil to think and whether it awakens his interest in applying his brain to the various problems and opportunities that life presents. If these have once been done, then factual knowledge can easily be assimilated. If these have not been done, then no amount of nodding acquaintance with widely varying fields of human knowledge will equip a boy or girl with an educated mind. We in England argue the case for specialization not primarily on the score of the information it provides but because it awakens interest, teaches clear thinking, and induces self-discipline in study.

31 We believe that, if you can find which of the recognized intellectual disciplines most arouses a boy's interest—and we confine his choice to five or six recognized disciplines, chosen for their intellectual content, not for their vocational value—if you can let him spend his time on what interests him, but insist that he must work hard at it, go deep into it, follow it up in the library or the laboratory, get around behind the stage scenery that defines the formal academic subject, you will really be teaching him how to use the mind that God has given him. This sort of intensive study takes a great deal of time, and that is why it can only be applied, for any one student, to a restricted range of subjects. No doubt you will say that the boy must be very narrow as a result. That may be. Are you sure that being narrow is worse than being shallow?

[Some of what Crowther says in these three paragraphs can't apply to you because you aren't—not yet, at least—a specialist. But as for the rest of it, how do you think it applies to the course you've been getting from this book? Have you been trying to learn a little bit of history, a little bit of psychology, a little bit of sociology, and so on?

Or have you been trying to learn to *think*—to learn how to use the mind that God has given you, as Crowther would put it? (Thinking, by the way, we might define or describe as the successful effort to see the relationship of ideas.)

In any case we have now reached Crowther's conclusion. Notice that in his next-to-last sentence he briefly alludes to his three main divisions, then in his last sentence applies them to an admirably diplomatic, yet quite honest, rounding off of his whole article.]

32 I find that English education has a high reputation among Americans. I am often asked, for example, whether it is not true that the eighteen-year-old boy in England is a year or two ahead of his American contemporary. I always answer that question, or assertion, by asking some others. What boy? If an English boy is still at school at eighteen, he is necessarily in the upper quartile in intelligence. Are you comparing him with the average American high school graduate, who is of average intelligence? And ahead in what? In the subjects to which he has been giving nearly all his time and attention for two years? It would be strange if he were not a long way ahead in those. Or over the whole range of a broad curriculum? He has been taught different things, by different methods, with a different purpose in view, in a different sort of school. There is no fair basis for a comparative judgment.

EXERCISE

Since this was originally an oral address, and since after study of it you understand it rather well, it is particularly suited for your reading aloud at home, *with expression*. And by expression I mean, principally, emphasizing items that come at the end and items that contrast.

chapter

In the following readings you will be on your own. But three suggestions may be appropriate.

First, do not suppose that you have *read* anything, if your reaction to it is that it is "uninteresting." Interest or lack of interest, excitement or boredom, stimulation or tedium—these are in the person, not the thing. Actually, you know this already: surely you are deeply interested in something that does not attract some friend of yours at all, and vice versa. Or you have lost interest in a pursuit that once absorbed you, or have acquired an interest in a subject that formerly did not appeal to you. "This doesn't interest me" is a conclusion far too easy—and immature. "Here's what the writer's explanation is" is a conclusion far harder, far more mature, and far more profitable.

Second, the writer will mention people and things that are unfamiliar to you. Does that say something—as you may have been unconsciously assuming—about those persons or things he mentions, or about *you*? (How significant that question is you have already realized from the alien vocabulary that writers seem, or once seemed, to be inflicting upon you.) Wise readers always recall Jacques Barzun's reminder that in one sense you read a book, but that in another sense the book reads *you*. Reflect as well that if the writer thought those

fourteen

on your own: additional readings

people and things worth mentioning, other writers may think them important, too—you may meet them again, they can begin to become familiar to you. If you pay attention to those persons and things now, you can begin to build up in your mind what has been called an "apperceptive mass": a stock or framework of knowledge into which you can fit other pieces of knowledge as they come along. For the head is not really like a pot: no, the more empty it is, the harder putting anything into it will be, whereas the fuller it is, the more you can put into it. It has the magic pitcher of the story beaten all hollow!

Third: though I personally disagree with some of the conceptions in a couple of the selections that follow, I have read and reread each article with profit. So do not read—at first—to agree or disagree. Do not indulge in the childish game of substituting "what you think" for the much harder question, the mature question, "what does the writer think?" The latter question is ultimately more rewarding, too, because you can hardly know what you think, or could think, unless you know why at least one other person thinks otherwise.

To sum up these three suggestions: avoid the slavery of having to exist, as a student, for what you read, by taking such pains in your reading that the articles you work on *begin to exist for you.*

LEARNING TO READ
Malcolm X

Malcolm X, a black civil rights activist, religious leader, writer, and speaker, was born Malcolm Little in Omaha, Nebraska, in 1925. Paroled from prison, he first joined the Black Muslims, then founded a new black organization, but was mysteriously assassinated at a New York rally in 1965. His Autobiography of Malcolm X *is well known, and he is widely revered.*

I became increasingly frustrated at not being able to express what I wanted to convey in letters that I wrote. In the street, I had been the most articulate hustler out there—I had commanded attention when I said something. But now, trying to write simple English, I not only wasn't articulate, I wasn't even functional. How would I sound writing in slang, the way I would *say* it, something such as, "Look, daddy, let me pull your coat about a cat, Elijah Muhammad—"

Every book I picked up had few sentences which didn't contain anywhere from one to nearly all of the words that might as well have been in Chinese. When I just skipped those words, of course, I really ended up with little idea of what the book said.

I saw that the best thing I could do was get hold of a dictionary—to study, to learn some words. I was lucky enough to reason also that I should try to improve my penmanship. It was sad. I couldn't even write in a straight line. It was both ideas together that moved me to request a dictionary along with some tablets and pencils from the Norfolk Prison Colony school.

I spent two days just riffling uncertainly through the dictionary's pages. I'd never realized so many words existed! I didn't know *which* words I needed to learn. Finally, just to start some kind of action, I began copying.

In my slow, painstaking, ragged handwriting, I copied into my tablet everything printed on that first page, down to the punctuation marks.

I believe it took me a day. Then, aloud, I read back, to myself, everything I'd written on the tablet. Over and over, aloud, to myself, I read my own handwriting.

I woke up the next morning, thinking about those words—immensely proud to realize that not only had I written so much at one time, but I'd written words that I never knew were in the world. Moreover, with a little effort, I also could remember what many of these words meant. I reviewed the words whose meanings I didn't remember. Funny thing, from the dictionary first page right now, that "aardvark" springs to my mind. The dictionary had a picture of it, a long-tailed, long-eared, burrowing African mammal, which lives off termites caught by sticking out its tongue as an anteater does for ants.

I was so fascinated that I went on—I copied the dictionary's next page. And the same experience came when I studied that. With every succeeding page, I also learned of people and places and events from history. Actually the dictionary is like a miniature encyclopedia. Finally the dictionary's A section had filled a whole tablet—and I went on into the B's. That was the way I started copying what eventually became the entire dictionary. It went a lot faster after so much practice helped me to pick up handwriting speed. Between what I wrote in my tablet, and writing letters, during the rest of my time in prison I would guess I wrote a million words.

I suppose it was inevitable that as my word-base broadened, I could for the first time pick up a book and read and now begin to understand what the book was saying. Anyone who has read a great deal can imagine the new world that opened. Let me tell you something: from then until I left that prison, in every free moment I had, if I was not reading in the library, I was reading on my bunk. You couldn't have gotten me out of my books with a wedge. Months passed without my even thinking about being imprisoned. In fact, up to then, I never had been so truly free in my life.

As you can imagine, especially in a prison where there was heavy emphasis on rehabilitation, an inmate was smiled upon if he demonstrated an unusually intense interest in books. There was a sizeable number of well-read inmates, especially the popular debaters. Some were said by many to be practically walking encyclopedias. They were almost celebrities. No university would ask any student to devour literature as I did when this new world opened to me, of being able to read and *understand*.

I have often reflected upon the new vistas that reading opened to me. I knew right there in prison that reading had changed forever the course of my life. As I see it today, the ability to read awoke inside me some long dormant craving to be mentally alive. I certainly wasn't seeking any degree, the way a college confers a status symbol upon its students. My homemade education gave me, with every additional book that I read, a little bit more sensitivity to the deafness, dumbness, and blindness that was afflicting the black race in America. Not long ago, an English writer telephoned me from London, asking questions. One was, "What's your alma mater?" I told him, "Books."

I told the Englishman that my alma mater was books, a good library. Every time I catch a plane, I have with me a book that I want to read—and that's a lot of books these days.

THREE DAYS TO SEE
Helen Keller

Born both blind and deaf, Helen Keller so far overrode this compound handicap as to become one of America's most widely read and enthusiastically admired women. The miracle of her education by Annie Sullivan was the subject of the play and film The Miracle Worker. *In her lectures in the United States, Europe, and the Orient, she helped not only the blind but also the sighted to see.*

If I were the president of a university I should establish a compulsory course in "How To Use Your Eyes." The professor would try to show his pupils how they could add joy to their lives by really seeing what passes unnoticed before them. He would try to awake their dormant and sluggish faculties.

Perhaps I can best illustrate by imagining what I should most like to see if I were given the use of my eyes, say, for just three days. And while I am imagining, suppose you, too, set your mind to work on the problem of how you would use your own eyes if you had only three more days to see. If with the oncoming darkness of the third night you knew that the sun would never rise for you again, how would you spend those three precious intervening days? What would you most want to let your gaze rest upon?

I, naturally, should want most to see the things which have become dear to me through my years of darkness. You, too, would want to let your eyes rest long on the things that have become dear to you so that you could take the memory of them with you into the night that loomed before you.

If, by some miracle, I were granted three seeing days, to be followed by a relapse into darkness, I should divide the period into three parts.

On the first day, I should want to see the people whose kindness and gentleness and companionship have made my life worth living. First I should like to gaze long upon the face of my dear teacher, Mrs. Anne Sullivan Macy, who came to me when I was a child and opened the outer world to me. I should want not merely to see the outline of her face, so that I could cherish it in my memory, but to study that face and find in it the living evidence of the sympathetic tenderness and patience with which she accomplished the difficult task of my education. I should like to see in her eyes that strength of character which has enabled her to stand firm in the face of difficulties, and that compassion for all humanity which she has revealed to me so often.

I do not know what it is to see into the heart of a friend through that "window of the soul," the eye. I can only "see" through my fingertips the outline of a face. I can detect laughter, sorrow, and many other obvious emotions. I know my friends from the feel of their faces. But I cannot really picture their personalities by touch. I know their personalities, of course, through other means, through the thoughts they express to me, through whatever of their actions are revealed to me. But I am denied that deeper understanding of them which I am sure would come through sight of them, through watching their reactions to various expressed thoughts and circumstances, through noting the immediate and fleeting reactions of their eyes and countenance.

Friends who are near to me I know well, because through the months and years they reveal themselves to me in all their phases; but of casual friends I have only an incomplete impression, an impression gained from a handclasp, from spoken words which I take from their lips with my fingertips, or which they tap into the palm of my hand.

How much easier, how much more satisfying it is for you who can see to grasp quickly the essential qualities of another person by watching the subtleties of expression, the quiver of a muscle, the flutter of a hand. But does it ever occur to you to use your sight to see into the inner nature of a friend or acquaintance? Do not most of you seeing people grasp casually the outward features of a face and let it go at that?

For instance, can you describe accurately the faces of five good friends? Some of you can, but many cannot. As an experiment, I have questioned husbands of long standing about the color of their wives' eyes, and often they express embarrassed confusion and admit that they do not know. And, incidentally, it is a chronic complaint of wives that their husbands do not notice new dresses, new hats, and changes in household arrangements.

The eyes of seeing persons soon become accustomed to the routine of their surroundings, and they actually see only the startling and spectacular. But even in viewing the most spectacular sights the eyes are lazy. Court records reveal every day how inaccurately "eyewitnesses" see. A given event will be "seen" in several different ways by as many witnesses. Some see more than others, but few see everything that is within the range of their vision.

Oh, the things that I should see if I had the power of sight for just three days!

The first day would be a busy one. I should call to me all my dear friends and look long into their faces, imprinting upon my mind the outward evidences of the beauty that is within them. I should let my eyes rest, too, on the face of a baby, so that I could catch a vision of the eager, innocent beauty which precedes the individual's consciousness of the conflicts which life develops.

And I should like to look into the loyal, trusting eyes of my dogs—the grave, canny little Scottie, Darkie, and the stalwart, understanding Great Dane, Helga, whose warm, tender, and playful friendships are so comforting to me.

On that busy first day I should also view the small simple things of my home. I want to see the warm colors in the rugs under my feet, the pictures on the walls, the intimate trifles that transform a house into home. My eyes would rest respectfully on the books in raised type which I have read, but they would be more eagerly interested in the printed books which seeing people can read, for during the long night of my life the books I have read and those which have been read to me have built themselves into a great shining lighthouse, revealing to me the deepest channels of human life and the human spirit.

In the afternoon of that first seeing day, I should take a long walk in the woods and intoxicate my eyes on the beauties of the world of Nature, trying desperately to absorb in a few hours the vast splendor which is constantly unfolding itself to those who can see. On the way home from my woodland jaunt my path would lie near a farm so that I might see the patient horses plowing in the field (perhaps I should see only a tractor!) and the serene content of men living close to the soil. And I should pray for the glory of a colorful sunset.

When dusk had fallen, I should experience the double delight of being able to see by artificial light, which the genius of man has created to extend the power of his sight when Nature decrees darkness.

In the night of that first day of sight, I should not be able to sleep, so full would be my mind of the memories of the day.

The next day—the second day of sight—I should arise with the dawn and see the thrilling miracle by which night is transformed into day. I should behold with awe the magnificent panorama of light with which the sun awakens the sleeping earth.

This day I should devote to a hasty glimpse of the world, past and present. I should want to see the pageant of man's progress, the kaleidoscope of the ages. How can so much be compressed into one day? Through the museums, of course. Often I have visited the New York Museum of Natural History to touch with my hands many of the objects there exhibited, but I have longed to see with my eyes the condensed history of the earth and its inhabitants displayed there—animals and the races of men pictured in their native environment; gigantic carcasses of dinosaurs and mastodons which roamed the earth long before man appeared, with his tiny stature and powerful brain, to conquer the animal kingdom; realistic presentations of the processes of evolution in animals, in man, and in the implements which man has used to fashion for himself a secure home on this planet; and a thousand and one other aspects of natural history.

I wonder how many readers of this article have viewed this panorama of the face of living things as pictured in that inspiring museum. Many, of course, have not had the opportunity, but I am sure that many who *have* had the opportunity have not made use of it. There, indeed, is a place to use your eyes. You who see can spend many fruitful days there, but I, with my imaginary three days of sight, could only take a hasty glimpse, and pass on.

My next stop would be the Metropolitan Museum of Art, for just as the Museum of Natural History reveals the material aspects of the world, so does the Metropolitan show the myriad facets of the human spirit. Throughout the history of humanity the urge to artistic expression has been almost as powerful as the urge for food, shelter, and procreation. And here, in the vast chambers of the Metropolitan Museum, is unfolded before me the spirit of Egypt, Greece, and Rome, as expressed in their art. I know well through my hands the sculptured gods and goddesses of the ancient Nile land. I have felt copies of Parthenon friezes, and I have sensed the rhythmic beauty of charging Athenian warriors. Apollos and Venuses and the Winged Victory of Samothrace are friends of my fingertips. The gnarled, bearded features of Homer are dear to me, for he, too, knew blindness.

My hands have lingered upon the living marble of Roman sculpture as well as that of later generations. I have passed my hands over a plaster cast of Michelangelo's inspiring and heroic Moses; I have sensed the power of Rodin; I have been awed by the devoted spirit of Gothic wood carving. These arts which can be touched have meaning for me, but even they were meant to be seen rather than felt, and I can only guess at the beauty which remains hidden from me. I can admire the simple lines of a Greek vase, but its figured decorations are lost to me.

So on this, my second day of sight, I should try to probe into the soul of man through his art. The things I knew through touch I should now see. More splendid still, the whole magnificent world of painting would be opened to me, from the Italian Primitives, with their serene religious devotion, to the Moderns, with their feverish visions. I should look deep into the canvases of Raphael, Leonardo da Vinci, Titian, Rembrandt. I should want to feast my eyes upon the warm colors of Veronese, study the mysteries of El Greco, catch a new vision of Nature from Corot. Oh, there is so much rich meaning and beauty in the art of the ages for you who have eyes to see!

Upon my short visit to this temple of art I should not be able to review a fraction of that great world of art which is open to you. I should be able to get only a superficial impression. Artists tell me that for a deep and true appreciation of art one must educate the eye. One must learn through experience to weigh the merits of line, of composition, of form and color. If I had eyes, how happily would I embark upon so fascinating a study! Yet I am told that, to many of you who have eyes to see, the world of art is a dark night, unexplored and unilluminated.

It would be with extreme reluctance that I should leave the Metropolitan Museum, which contains the key to beauty—a beauty so neglected. Seeing persons, however, do not need a Metropolitan to find this key to beauty. The same key lies waiting in smaller museums, and in books on the shelves of even small libraries. But naturally, in my limited time of imaginary sight, I should choose the place where the key unlocks the greatest treasures in the shortest time.

The evening of my second day of sight I should spend at a theater or at the movies. Even now I often attend theatrical performances of all sorts, but the action of the play must be spelled into my hand by a companion. But how I should like to see with my own eyes the fascinating figure of Hamlet, or the gusty Falstaff amid colorful Elizabethan trappings! How I should like to follow each movement of the graceful Hamlet, each strut of the hearty Falstaff! And since I could see only one play, I should be confronted by the many-horned dilemma, for there are scores of plays I should want to see. You who have eyes can see any you like. How many of you, I wonder, when you gaze at a play, a movie, or any spectacle, realize and give thanks for the miracle of sight which enables you to enjoy its color, grace, and movement?

I cannot enjoy the beauty of rhythmic movement except in a sphere restricted to the touch of my hands. I can vision only dimly the grace of a Pavlova, although I know something of the delight of rhythm, for often I can sense the beat of music as it vibrates through the floor. I can well imagine that cadenced motion must be one of the most pleasing sights in the world. I have been able to gather something of this by tracing with my fingers the lines in sculptured marble; if this static grace can be so lovely, how much more acute must be the thrill of seeing grace in motion.

One of my dearest memories is of the time when Joseph Jefferson allowed me to touch his face and hands as he went through some of the gestures and speeches of his beloved Rip Van Winkle. I was able to catch thus a meager glimpse of the world of drama, and I shall never forget the delight of that moment. But, oh, how much I must miss, and how much pleasure you seeing ones can derive from watching and hearing the interplay of speech and movement in the unfolding of a dramatic performance! If I could see only one play, I should know how to picture in my mind the action of a hundred plays which I have read or had transferred to me through the medium of the manual alphabet.

So, through the evening of my second imaginary day of sight, the great figures of dramatic literature would crowd sleep from my eyes.

The following morning, I should again greet the dawn, anxious to discover new delights, for I am sure that, for those who have eyes which really see, the dawn of each day must be a perpetually new revelation of beauty.

This, according to the terms of my imagined miracle, is to be my third and last day of sight. I shall have no time to waste in regrets or longings; there is too much to see. The first day I devoted to my friends, animate and inanimate. The second revealed to me the history of man and Nature. Today I shall spend in the workaday world of the present, amid the haunts of men going about the business of life. And where can one find so many activities and conditions of men as in New York? So the city becomes my destination.

I start from my home in the quiet little suburb of Forest Hills, Long Island. Here, surrounded by green lawns, trees, and flowers, are neat little houses, happy with the voices and movements of wives and children, havens of peaceful rest for men who toil in the city. I drive across the lacy structure of steel which spans the East River, and I get a new and startling vision of the power and ingenuity of the mind of man. Busy boats chug and scurry about the river—racy speedboats, stolid, snorting tugs. If I had long days of sight ahead, I should spend many of them watching the delightful activity upon the river.

I look ahead, and before me rise the fantastic towers of New York, a city that seems to have stepped from the pages of a fairy story. What an awe-inspiring sight, these glittering spires, these vast banks of stone and steel— structures such as the gods might build for themselves! This animated picture is a part of the lives of millions of people every day. How many, I wonder, give it so much as a second glance? Very few, I fear. Their eyes are blind to this magnificent sight because it is so familiar to them.

I hurry to the top of one of those gigantic structures, the Empire State Building, for there, a short time ago, I "saw" the city below through the eyes of my secretary. I am anxious to compare my fancy with reality. I am sure I should not be disappointed in the panorama spread out before me, for to me it would be a vision of another world.

Now I begin my rounds of the city. First, I stand at a busy corner, merely looking at people, trying by sight of them to understand something of their lives. I see smiles, and I am happy. I see determination, and I am proud. I see suffering, and I am compassionate.

I stroll down Fifth Avenue. I throw my eyes out of focus so that I see no particular object but only a seething kaleidoscope of color. I am certain that the colors of women's dresses moving in a throng must be a gorgeous spectacle of which I should never tire. But perhaps if I had sight I should be like most other women—too interested in styles and the cut of individual dresses to give much attention to the splendor of color in the mass. And I am convinced, too, that I should become an inveterate window shopper, for it must be a delight to the eye to view the myriad articles of beauty on display.

From Fifth Avenue I make a tour of the city—to Park Avenue, to the slums, to factories, to parks where children play. I take a stay-at-home trip abroad by visiting the foreign quarters. Always my eyes are open wide to all the sights of both happiness and misery so that I may probe deep and add to my understanding of how people work and live. My heart is full of the images of people and things. My eye passes lightly over no single trifle; it strives to touch and hold closely each thing its gaze rests upon. Some sights are pleasant, filling the heart with happiness; but some are miserably pathetic. To these latter I do not shut my eyes, for they, too, are part of life. To close the eye on them is to close the heart and mind.

My third day of sight is drawing to an end. Perhaps there are many serious pursuits to which I should devote the few remaining hours, but I am afraid that on the evening of that last day I should again run away to the theater, to a hilariously funny play, so that I might appreciate the overtones of comedy in the human spirit.

At midnight my temporary respite from blindness would cease, and permanent night would close in on me again. Naturally in those three short days I should not have seen all I wanted to see. Only when darkness had again descended upon me should I realize how much I had left unseen. But my mind would be so crowded with glorious memories that I should have little time for regrets. Thereafter the touch of every object would bring a glowing memory of how that object looked.

Perhaps this short outline of how I should spend three days of sight does not agree with the program you would set for yourself if you knew that you were about to be stricken blind. I am, however, sure that if you actually faced that fate your eyes would open to things you had never seen before, storing up memories for the long night ahead. You would use your eyes as never before. Everything you saw would become dear to you. Your eyes would touch and embrace every object that came within your range of vision. Then, at last, you would really see, and a new world of beauty would open itself before you.

I who am blind can give one hint to those who see—one admonition to those who would make full use of the gift of sight: Use your eyes as if tomorrow you would be stricken blind. And the same method can be applied to the other senses. Hear the music of voices, the song of a bird, the mighty strains of an orchestra, as if you would be stricken deaf tomorrow. Touch each object you want to touch as if tomorrow your tactile sense would fail. Smell the perfume of flowers, taste with relish each morsel, as if tomorrow you could never smell and taste again. Make the most of every sense; glory in all the facets of pleasure and beauty which the world reveals to you through the several means of contact which Nature provides. But of all the senses, I am sure that sight must be the most delightful.

THE CASE FOR BASIC EDUCATION
Clifton Fadiman

Clifton Fadiman exemplifies what used to be called "a man of letters." As a teacher, a writer, and a lecturer, he has attempted to promote better reading and writing habits in the country at large. His long association as a member of the selection committee for the Book-of-the-Month Club is just one example of the importance he attaches to reading books. What follows is the conclusion of Fadiman's introductory essay to a collection of papers, The Case for Basic Education, *edited by Dr. James D. Koerner.*

I am a very lucky man, for I believe that my generation was just about the last one to receive an undiluted basic education. As this is written, I am fifty-four years old. Thus I received my secondary school education from 1916 to 1920. Though I was not well educated by European standards, I was very well educated by present-day American ones. For this I am grateful to my country, my city, and my teachers. Of personal credit I can claim little.

My high school was part of the New York City system. It had no amenities. Its playground was asphalt and about the size of two large drawing rooms. It looked like a barracks. It made no provision for dramatics or square dancing. It didn't even have a psychiatrist—perhaps because we didn't need one. The students were all from what is known as the "underprivileged"—or what we used to call poor—class. Today this class is depended on to provide the largest quota of juvenile delinquents. During my four years in high school there was one scandalous case in which a student stole a pair of rubbers.

Academically my school was neither very good nor very bad. The same was true of me. As the area of elective subjects was strictly limited, I received approximately the same education my fellows did. (Unfortunately Latin was not compulsory: I had to learn it—badly—by myself later on.) Here is what—in addition to the standard minors of drawing, music, art and gym—I was taught some forty years ago:

Four years of English, including rigorous drill in composition, formal grammar and public speaking.

Four years of German.

Three years of French.

Three or four years (I am not sure which) of history, including classical, European and American, plus a no-nonsense factual course in civics, which was dull but at least didn't pretend to be a "social science."

One year of physics.

One year of biology.

Three years of mathematics, through trigonometry.

That, or its near equivalent, was the standard high school curriculum in New York forty years ago. That was all I learned, all any of us learned, all all of us learned. All these subjects can be, and often are, better taught today—when they are taught at all on this scale. However, I was taught French and German well enough so that in later years I made part of my living as a translator. I was taught rhetoric and composition well enough to make it possible for me to become a practicing journalist. I was taught public speaking well enough to enable me to replace my lower-class accent with at least a passable one; and I learned also the rudiments of enunciation, placing, pitch, and proper breathing so that in after years I found it not too difficult to get odd jobs as a public lecturer and radio-and-television handyman.

I adduce these practical arguments only to explode them. They may seem important to the life-adjuster. They are not important to me. One can make a living without French. One can even make a living without a knowledge of spelling. And it is perfectly possible to rise to high estate without any control whatsoever over the English language.

What *is* important about this old-fashioned basic education (itself merely a continuation and sophistication of the basic education then taught in the primary schools) is not that it prepared me for life or showed me how to get along with my fellow men. Its importance to me and, I believe, to most of my fellow students, irrespective of their later careers, is twofold:

(1) It furnished me with a foundation on which later on, within the limits of my abilities, I could erect any intellectual structure I fancied. It gave me the wherewithal for the self-education that should be every man's concern to the hour of his death.

(2) It precluded my ever becoming Lost. . . .

I want now to explain (2) because the explanation should help to make clear why in our time basic education is needed not only in principle but as a kind of emergency measure.

Again I hope the reader will forgive the intrusion of the autobiographical note.

Considered as a well-rounded American I am an extremely inferior product. I am a poor mechanic. I play no games beyond a little poorish tennis and I haven't played that for five years. I swim, type, dance and drive raggedly, though, with respect to the last, I hope non-dangerously. I have had to learn about sex and marriage without benefit of classroom instruction. I would like to be well-rounded and I admire those who are. But it is too late. I take no pleasure in my inferiorities but I accept the fact that I must live with them.

I feel inferior. Well and good. It seems to hurt nobody. But, though I feel inferior, I do not feel Lost. I have not felt lost since being graduated from high school. I do not expect ever to feel lost. This is not because I am wise, for I am not. It is not because I am learned, for I am not. It is not because I have mastered the art of getting along with my peers, for I do not know the first thing about it. I am often terrified by the world I live in, often horrified, usually unequal to its challenges. But I am not lost in it.

I know how I came to be an American citizen in 1959; what large general movements of history produced me; what my capacities and limitations are; what truly interests me; and how valuable or valueless these interests are. My tastes are fallible but not so fallible that I am easily seduced by the vulgar and transitory—though often enough I am unequal to a proper appreciation of the noble and the permanent. In a word, like tens of millions of others in this regard, I feel at home in the world. I am at times scared but I can truthfully say that I am not bewildered.

I do not owe this to any superiority of nature. I owe it, I sincerely believe, to the conventional basic education I received beginning about a half century ago. It taught me how to read, write, speak, calculate, and listen. It taught me the elements of reasoning and it put me on to the necessary business of drawing abstract conclusions from particular instances. It taught me how to locate myself in time and space and to survey the present in the light of an imperfect but ever-functioning knowledge of the past. It provided me with great models by which to judge my own lesser performances. And it gave me the ability to investigate for myself anything that interested me, provided my mind was equal to it.

I admit this is not much. But it is something, and that a vital something. And that something—here we touch the heart of our discussion—is becoming ever rarer among the products of our present educational system.

The average high school graduate today is just as intelligent as my fellow students were. He is just as educable. But he is Lost, in greater or less degree.

By that I mean he feels little relation to the whole world in time and space, and only the most formal relation to his own country. He may "succeed," he may become a good, law-abiding citizen, he may produce other good, law-abiding citizens, and on the whole he may live a pleasant—that is, not painful—life. Yet during most of that life, and particularly after his fortieth year or so, he will feel vaguely disconnected, rootless, purposeless. Like the very plague he will shun any searching questions as to his own worth, his own identity. He will die after having lived a fractional life.

Is this what he really wants? Perhaps it is. It all comes round again to what was said at the opening of these remarks. Again it depends on one's particular vision of man. If we see our youngster as an animal whose main function is biological and social adaptation on virtually a day-to-day basis, then his fractional life is not fractional at all. It is total. But in that case our school curriculum should reflect our viewpoint. It should include the rudiments of reading so that our high school graduate may decipher highway markers, lavatory signs, and perhaps the headlines of some undemanding newspaper. It should include a large number of electives, changing every year, that may be of use to him in job hunting. And primarily it should include as much play and sport as possible, for these are the proper activities of animals, and our boy is an animal.

Yet the doubt persists. *Is* this really what he wants? And once again the answer depends on our faith. For example, the "Rockefeller Report" on Education (published in 1958 and called *The Pursuit of Excellence*) did not issue, except indirectly, from surveys, analyses, polls or statistical abstracts. It issued from faith. The following sentences do not comprise a scientific conclusion. They are an expression of faith, like the Lord's Prayer:

"What most people, young or old, want is not merely security or comfort or luxury—although they are glad enough to have these. They want meaning in their lives. If their era and their culture and their leaders do not or cannot offer them great meanings, great objectives, great convictions, then they will settle for shallow and trivial meanings."

There is no compulsion to believe this. If we do not believe it, and unqualifiedly, there is no case for basic education. Which means that, except for the superior intellect, there is no case for traditional education at all. In that event we should at once start to overhaul our school system in the light of a conception of man that sees him as a continually adjusting, pleasure-seeking, pain-avoiding animal.

But if we do believe it, and unqualifiedly, then the proposals contained in this book might at least be considered as guidelines, subject to discussion and modification.

The root of our trouble does not lie in an unbalanced curriculum, or in an inadequate emphasis on any one subject, or in poor teaching methods, or in insufficient facilities, or in underpaid instructors. It lies in the circumstance that somehow the average high school graduate does not know who he is, where he is, or how he got there. It lies in the fact that naturally enough he "will settle for shallow and trivial meanings." If nothing in his early education has convinced him that Newton, Shakespeare and Lincoln are both more interesting and more admirable than Frank Sinatra, Jerry Lewis and Pat Boone, he will find answers to his questions in Sinatra, Lewis and Boone, and not in Newton, Shakespeare and Lincoln. If he has learned little or no history, geography, science, mathematics, foreign languages, or English he will, naturally enough, learn (for even if all men do not desire to know, in Aristotle's sense, surely they desire to know *something*) golf, quail-shooting, barbecuing, and some specialized technique of buying and selling.

In accordance with his luck and his temperament, he may become happily lost, or unhappily lost. But lost he will become. Lost he will remain. Lost he will die.

And if we allow these lost ones to multiply indefinitely, they will see to it that our country is lost also.

CETI

Lewis Thomas

"One of the best writers of the short essay in English," in a Newsweek *reviewer's estimate, and a* New Yorker *poet, Lewis Thomas, M.D., has taught and researched in many of the nation's foremost medical institutions and now heads the Memorial Sloan-Kettering Cancer Center. He believes that all scientific research, even without immediate results, is valuable, and that "what must be planned for is the totally unforeseeable."*

Tau Ceti is a relatively nearby star that sufficiently resembles our sun to make its solar system a plausible candidate for the existence of life. We are, it appears, ready to begin getting in touch with Ceti, and with any other interested celestial body in more remote places, out to the edge. CETI is also, by intention, the acronym of the First International Conference on Communication with Extraterrestrial Intelligence, held in 1972 in Soviet Armenia under the joint sponsorship of the National Academy of Sciences of the United States and the Soviet Academy, which involved eminent physicists and astronomers from various countries, most of whom are convinced that the odds for the existence of life elsewhere are very high, with a reasonable probability that there are civilizations, one place or another, with technologic mastery matching or exceeding ours.

On this assumption, the conferees thought it likely that radioastronomy would be the generally accepted mode of interstellar communication, on grounds of speed and economy. They made a formal recommendation that we organize an international cooperative program, with new and immense radio telescopes, to probe the reaches of deep space for electromagnetic signals making sense. Eventually, we would plan to send out messages on our own and receive answers, but at the outset it seems more practical to begin by catching snatches of conversation between others.

So, the highest of all our complex technologies in the hardest of our sciences will soon be engaged, full scale, in what is essentially biologic research—and with some aspects of social science, at that.

The earth has become, just in the last decade, too small a place. We have the feeling of being confined—shut in; it is something like outgrowing a small town in a small county. The views of the dark, pocked surface of Mars, still lifeless to judge from the latest photographs, do not seem to have extended our reach; instead, they bring closer, too close, another unsatisfactory feature of our local environment. The blue noonday sky, cloudless, has lost its old look of immensity. The word is out that the sky is not limitless; it is finite. It is, in truth, only a kind of local roof, a membrane under which we live, luminous but confusingly refractile when suffused with sunlight; we can sense its concave surface a few miles over our heads. We know that it is tough and thick enough so that when hard objects strike it from the outside they burst into flames. The color photographs of the earth are more amazing than anything outside: we live inside a blue chamber, a bubble of air blown by ourselves. The other sky beyond, absolutely black and appalling, is wide-open country, irresistible for exploration.

Here we go, then. An extraterrestrial embryologist, having a close look at us from time to time, would probably conclude that the morphogenesis of the earth is coming along well, with the beginnings of a nervous system and fair-size ganglions in the form of cities, and now with specialized, dish-shaped sensory organs, miles across, ready to receive stimuli. He may well wonder, however, how we will go about responding. We are evolving into the situation of a Skinner pigeon in a Skinner box, peering about in all directions, trying to make connections, probing.

When the first word comes in from outer space, finally, we will probably be used to the idea. We can already provide a quite good explanation for the origin of life, here or elsewhere. Given a moist planet with methane, formaldehyde, ammonia, and some usable minerals, all of which abound, exposed to lightning or ultraviolet irradiation at the right temperature, life might start off almost anywhere. The tricky, unsolved thing is how to get the polymers to arrange in membanes and invent replication. The rest is clear going. If they follow our protocol, it will be anaerobic life at first, then photosynthesis and the first exhalation of oxygen, then respiring life and the great burst of variation, then speciation, and, finally, some kind of consciousness. It is easy, in the telling.

I suspect that when we have recovered from the first easy acceptance of signs of life from elsewhere, and finished nodding at each other, and finished smiling, we will be in shock. We have had it our way, relatively speaking, being unique all these years, and it will be hard to deal with the thought that the whole, infinitely huge, spinning, clocklike apparatus around us is itself animate, and can sprout life whenever the conditions are right. We will respond, beyond doubt, by making connections after the fashion of established life, floating out our filaments, extending pili, but we will end up feeling smaller than ever, as small as a single cell, with a quite new sense of continuity. It will take some getting used to.

The immediate problem, however, is a much more practical down-to-earth matter, and must be giving insomnia to the CETI participants. Let us assume that there is, indeed, sentient life in one or another part of remote space, and that we will be successful in getting in touch with it. What on earth are we going to talk about? If, as seems likely, it is a hundred or more light years away, there are going to be some very long pauses. The barest amenities, on which we rely for opening conversations—Hello, are you there? from us, followed by Yes, hello, from them—will take two hundred years at least. By the time we have our party we may have forgotten what we had in mind.

We could begin by gambling on the rightness of our technology and just send out news of ourselves, like a mimeographed Christmas letter, but we would have to choose our items carefully, with durability of meaning in mind. Whatever information we provide must still make sense to us two centuries later, and must still seem important, or the conversation will be an embarrassment to all concerned. In two hundred years it is, as we have found, easy to lose the thread.

Perhaps the safest thing to do at the outset, if technology permits, is to send music. This language may be the best we have for explaining what we are like to others in space, with least ambiguity. I would vote for Bach, all of Bach, streamed out into space, over and over again. We would be bragging, of course, but it is surely excusable for us to put the best possible face on at the beginning of such an acquaintance. We can tell the harder truths later. And, to do ourselves justice, music would give a fairer picture of what we are really like than some of the other things we might be sending, like *Time,* say, or a history of the U.N. or Presidential speeches. We could send out our science, of course, but just think of the wincing at this end when the polite comments arrive two hundred years from now. Whatever we offer as today's items of liveliest interest are bound to be out of date and irrelevant, maybe even ridiculous. I think we should stick to music.

Perhaps, if the technology can be adapted to it, we should send some paintings. Nothing would better describe what this place is like, to an outsider, than the Cézanne demonstrations that an apple is really part fruit, part earth.

What kinds of questions should we ask? The choices will be hard, and everyone will want his special question first. What are your smallest particles? Did you think yourselves unique? Do you have colds? Have you anything quicker than light? Do you always tell the truth? Do you cry? There is no end to the list.

Perhaps we should wait a while, until we are sure we know what we want to know, before we get down to detailed questions. After all, the main question will be the opener: Hello, are you there? If the reply should turn out to be Yes, hello, we might want to stop there and think about that, for quite a long time.

CELESTIAL NAVIGATION BY BIRDS

E. G. F. Sauer

The German ornithologist E. G. F. Sauer conducted his experiments on migration at the University of Freiburg, where he has since been appointed dozent in the natural science faculty. He grew up in Germany's Black Forest, where he acquired his interest in the habits of birds.

In spring and summer the songbirds known as the warblers are familiar residents in the countries throughout Europe. City dwellers know them well, for the small, gray birds find a home to their liking in the shrubs and hedges of gardens and small parks. During the spring breeding season the air is filled with their loud, melodic singing as each male establishes a small territory for himself in noisy battle with a rival. Once the claims are decided, the truculence and the songs subside; the birds proceed to mate and to raise their young. In late summer they feed amicably on elderberries and blackberries and they flit about in peace among the bushes. Then in August the birds begin to grow restless; their migratory instinct stirs. Suddenly, in one night, the whole resident population of one species is off and away. The next morning the bushes are filled with a new lot of warblers that have flown in from more northern areas; they stay for a few days and then they too fly on to the south. Through the weeks of September and October there is a continuous coming and going of hordes of the migrating warblers. Gradually the number passing through diminishes. The species called the garden warblers disappears first, then the whitethroats, after them the lesser whitethroats, and finally the blackcaps.

Where do they go? Ornithologists know exactly where the warblers go, for they have banded these birds for many years and followed them to their winter homes. With the exception of some blackcaps, these warblers travel to various parts of Africa. Some of them migrate as far as from Scandinavia to the southern part of Africa—a distance of seven thousand miles and more. In the spring the birds migrate back to the same place that they left in the fall.

Most remarkable of all is that each bird finds its own way to its destination! The warblers do not follow a leader or make the journey as a group; they navigate individually. And young birds making their first migration reach their goal as surely as the experienced travelers. Somehow, purely by instinct, the warblers know exactly how to set their course.

The navigation powers of birds have fascinated investigators for more than a century. By now there is a large literature of well-documented testimony to their amazing performances. The late Werner Rüppell of Germany, one of the leading experimenters on bird migration, found that starlings taken from their nests near Berlin and carried away to all points of the compass would find their way back to their nesting places from as far as 1,250 miles away. The Manx Shearwater, a sea bird, has astonished investigators with still more spectacular feats; one shearwater, taken from the west coast of England by G. V. T. Matthews and flown by plane to Boston, was back in its English nest in 12 days, having winged its own way 3,067 miles across the unknown Atlantic. The Pacific golden plover migrates each fall from its breeding grounds along the Bering sea coast to its winter home in the Hawaiian Islands. This bird, lacking webbed feet, cannot rest on the water as waterfowl do; it must fly on steadily for several days to reach its destination over thousands of miles of ocean. If it wandered only slightly off course, it would become lost and exhausted in the vast Pacific, but it finds its way unerringly to Hawaii.

Until recently attempts to explain the incredible navigation feats of birds were almost entirely a matter of speculation. Various theorists proposed that the birds were guided by the earth's magnetic field, by the Coriolis force arising from the earth's rotation, by landmarks, and so on. But more and more ornithologists have been driven to the conclusion that birds must rely mainly on celestial navigation—the sun by day, the constellations by night.

The idea that birds are guided by the sun was suggested as long as half a century ago, but it was not taken seriously until the early 1950's, when experimenters began to turn up some interesting evidence. Gustav Kramer in Germany and G. V. T. Matthews in England discovered independently that homing pigeons and wild birds can use the sun as a compass and that they possess a "time sense" which allows them to take account of the sun's motion across the sky. Other zoologists have confirmed these findings. It has now been proved, in fact, that our warblers can orient themselves by the sun.

But the warblers fly mainly at night. What sort of system do they use to steer their course in their nocturnal migrations nearly halfway around the globe? Several years ago the author and his wife started a systematic laboratory study of this question by means of specially designed cages in our aviary at Freiburg.

We had already seen laboratory proof of the stirring of the migratory instinct in these small world-travelers and of a seasonal time sense that governed this urge. We had hatched and raised warblers in completely closed, sound-proof chambers where they lived in the illusion of eternal summer, year in and year out. Yet, although they seemed to have no outward cues of the yearly rhythm of nature, in the autumn the birds would begin to flit restlessly from branch to branch or flutter continually over their perches, night after wakeful night. They kept this up for many weeks—about the length of time it would have taken them to fly to Africa. Then they went back to sleeping again at night. In the spring, about the time that warblers migrate back from Africa to their European homes, our birds again had a spell of restless, wakeful nights. It was as if they had an inner clock which told them when the time had come to take wing for distant parts.

To explore the orientation question we now placed warblers in a cage with a glass opening at the top, so that they could see part of the sky (but nothing else of their surroundings). At the season of migration the birds would begin to flutter and, peculiarly enough, each would take up a position pointing in a particular geographic direction, like the needle of a compass. Even when we tried to turn the birds away by rotating their ring-shaped perch, they stubbornly turned back to the preferred direction. The direction in each case was characteristic of the species: the garden warblers, the whitethroats, and the blackcaps all pointed toward the southwest, the lesser whitethroats toward the southeast (that is, in the fall; in the spring these directions were reversed). Now these are precisely the directions in which the respective species start their migrations from central Europe to Africa! The lesser whitethroats start southeastward, flying across the Balkans, and then turn south up the Nile Valley; the other species all take off southwestward and fly to Africa by way of Spain and Gibraltar.

Experienced or inexperienced, the birds invariably took up the appropriate direction of flight in the cage. How did they know the direction? Seemingly the only clue available to them was the starry night sky overhead. To explore this theory further we now put them through a series of tests. We found that when the stars were hidden by thick clouds, the birds became completely disoriented. They were likewise confused when only diffuse and strongly polarized light came through their skylight. To adopt and keep to a definite direction they needed a look at the starry sky. Indeed, the birds watched the sky so intently that shooting stars made them change their direction for a short time.

For still more rigidly controlled experiments we proceeded to test the birds in a cage placed in a planetarium: that is, with a dome showing an artificial replica of the natural starry sky. Again, when the dome was merely illuminated with diffuse light (showing no stars), the warblers were unable to choose a preferred direction. But when the planetarium sky matched the local night sky, the birds took up the proper direction just as if they were seeing the natural sky, but now adjusted to the artificial planetarium directions.

Now our artificial dome permitted us to shift the stars and constellations about. By changing the north-south declination (height) of the stars we could change the apparent geographical latitude, making the birds believe that they were farther south or north than they actually were. Similarly by shifting the sky in the east-west direction we might mislead the birds about their position in longitude. How would they behave under these circumstances?

To illustrate the results I shall describe some experiments with a lesser whitethroat warbler. Recall that the lesser whitethroat normally first travels southeastward across the Balkans and then turns due south, flying along the Nile to its winter home in the region of the Nile headwaters. In our experiments it turned out that as long as the planetarium sky was adjusted to the latitudes of 50 to 40 degrees north, this bird took up the expected flight position facing southeast. But as we shifted the sky, simulating more southerly latitudes, the bird tended to turn more and more toward the southern direction, until, at the latitude of 15 degrees, it set its couse due south!

In other words, this lesser whitethroat, which had spent all its life in a cage and never traveled under a natural sky, let alone migrated to Africa, still displayed an inborn ability to use the guidance of the stars to follow the usual route of its species, adjusting its direction nicely at each given latitude. Earlier investigators had supposed that these birds used landmarks to find their route: for example, that the coastline at the eastern end of the Mediterranean was the cue which told them to turn south. But our experiments proved that the birds are able to do it only by the stars.

Now let us see what happened when we shifted the planetarium sky to change the longitude, or, corresponding to it, the time. One night, while the lesser whitethroat was flapping its wings and heading in the southeast direction, we suddenly presented the bird with a sky shifted to the configuration five hours and 10 minutes ahead of the local time; in other words, the apparent geographical position of the cage then corresponded to a point 77.5 degrees eastward in longitude at this particular time. The bird at once showed that it was deeply disturbed. It looked excitedly at the unfamiliar sky and for almost a full minute stood irresolutely. Then it suddenly turned and took wing in the westward direction. According to the sky, its position at the moment corresponded to a point near Lake Balkhash in Siberia; the bird, to correct its displacement, was heading directly toward the usual migration starting point in Europe.

As we reduced its displacement, the bird shifted its heading more and more from due west toward the south. When the displacement was only an hour, corresponding to a position near Vienna, the lesser whitethroat headed south; when the canopy of stars was restored to the correct configuration at our locality for the season and time of night, the bird took up the normal heading toward the southeast.

The behavior of this individual, confirmed by experiments with other birds, leaves no doubt that the warblers have a remarkable hereditary mechanism for orienting themselves by the stars—a detailed image of the starry configuration of the sky coupled with a precise time sense which relates the heavenly canopy to the geography of the earth at every time and season. At their very first glimpse of the sky the birds automatically know the right direction. Without benefit of previous experience, with no cue except the stars, the birds are able to locate themselves in time and space and to find their way to their destined homes.

To be sure, the warblers do not have to rely solely on the constellations. In daytime they can guide themselves by the position of the sun. On cloudy nights they get some guidance from mountain ranges, coastlines, and river courses gleaming in the pale night shine. Only in almost total darkness, when thick clouds utterly hide the sky, are the birds in trouble: they circle helplessly and often are drawn to lighthouses.

We are going on to study the warblers' orientation system in more detail, systematically removing constellations or stars from our planetarium sky one by one to see if we can reduce the guidance cues to a basic pattern. One very interesting puzzle is the fact that the birds must somehow be able to make adjustments to astronomical evolution, for in the course of time the pattern of constellations in the sky is slowly but constantly changing. Even more difficult to explain is the mystery of how the birds ever came to rely on celestial navigation and to develop their skill in the first place. We know that the warblers are not the only creatures possessing this gift: other birds, fish, insects, crabs, and spiders have been found by experiment to be capable of guiding themselves by the sun. But there are many other guidance mechanisms and signposts available on earth. What evolutionary process was it that endowed these animals with the highly sophisticated ability to read the stars?

Whatever the answer, we cannot help marveling at the wondrous celestial instinct of the warblers. When fall comes, the little garden warbler, weighing barely three quarters of an ounce, sets off one night on an unbelievable journey. All alone, never in the collective security of a flock, it wings its solitary way southwestward over Germany, France, and Spain, and then swings south to its distant goal in southern Africa. It flies on unerringly, covering a hundred miles and more in a single night, never once stopping in its course, certain of its goal. When drifted by heavy sidewinds, the bird navigates back to its primary course in the next calm night. In the spring it takes off again and northward retraces its path to its nesting place in a European thicket—there to give birth to a new generation of little warblers which will grow up, without being taught, with the self-same capacity to follow the same route across the continents and oceans by the map of the stars.

I believe it is the great critic Irving Howe who tells the story. In the old days in the United States, when cigars were rolled in small shops by hand, each cigar maker being paid per cigar rolled, in many shops they found how to occupy their time during their mechanical routine. They would choose one member from their dozen or so workers to leave off rolling cigars, post himself at the front of the shop, and read to them (each then contributing to him a quota of rolled cigars).

What did he read to them? Well, for instance, the works of German economists! Those men had never had a course in reading. Indeed I wonder how many of them had gone even as far as the eighth grade. How did they do it? By *paying attention*, by being determined to follow the line of thought and grasp the point.

A friend who conscientiously read, and reread, a prepublication

afterword

version of this book, and then sent valuable suggestions and encouragement, contributes a similar story. He recalls an article by Huey Newton in which he relates how he taught himself to read in prison using the writings of Plato and Aristotle. There is really difficult explanatory prose for you, but Huey Newton obviously taught himself to pay strict attention and doggedly follow a line of thought.

You, as time goes on, may not consciously remember the individual techniques by which you learned in this book to take the step ahead that those cigar makers and Huey Newton had to take unaided, and far more laboriously. But if you retain from this book simply the encouragement to pay attention—to determine to read *for the point*—you have set your foot firmly on the road that will lead you to become, eventually, a mature and accomplished reader.

141